FAITH GORSKY AND **LARA CLEVENGER,** MSH, RDN, CPT

KETO BREAD

FROM BAGELS AND BUNS TO CRUSTS AND MUFFINS, 100 LOW-CARB, KETO-FRIENDLY BREADS FOR EVERY MEAL

ADAMS MEDIA

NEW YORK LONDON TORONTO SYDNEY NEW DELHI

Adams Media
An Imprint of Simon & Schuster, Inc.
57 Littlefield Street
Avon, Massachusetts 02322

First Adams Media trade paperback edition September 2019

ADAMS MEDIA and colophon are trademarks of Simon & Schuster.

For information about special discounts for bulk purchases, please contact Simon & Schuster Special Sales at 1-866-506-1949 or business@simonandschuster.com.

The Simon & Schuster Speakers Bureau can bring authors to your live event. For more information or to book an event contact the Simon & Schuster Speakers Bureau at 1-866-248-3049 or visit our website at www.simonspeakers.com.

Interior design by Sylvia McArdle and Stephanie Hannus
Interior photographs by James Stefiuk, Faith Gorsky, and Lara Clevenger

Manufactured in the United States of America

10 9 8 7 6 5 4 3 2

Library of Congress Cataloging-in-Publication Data has been applied for.

ISBN 978-1-5072-1090-1
ISBN 978-1-5072-1091-8 (ebook)

Many of the designations used by manufacturers and sellers to distinguish their products are claimed as trademarks. Where those designations appear in this book and Simon & Schuster, Inc., was aware of a trademark claim, the designations have been printed with initial capital letters.

Always follow safety and commonsense cooking protocols while using kitchen utensils, operating ovens and stoves, and handling uncooked food. If children are assisting in the preparation of any recipe, they should always be supervised by an adult.

The information in this book should not be used for diagnosing or treating any health problem. Not all diet and exercise plans suit everyone. You should always consult a trained medical professional before starting a diet, taking any form of medication, or embarking on any fitness or weight-training program. The author and publisher disclaim any liability arising directly or indirectly from the use of this book.

CONTENTS

CHAPTER 3
BREAKFAST 59

CHAPTER 4
LUNCH 79

CHAPTER 5
DINNER 97

CHAPTER 6

SNACKS 127

CHAPTER 7

DESSERTS 153

INTRODUCTION

Biscuits.

Waffles.

Muffins.

Crackers.

Cakes.

Cookies.

If you thought you'd have to give all this up just to be successful on the keto diet, think again! *Keto Bread* will reinvent pizza night, transform birthday cake, bring the beloved sandwich back into your life, and give you tons of keto options for both family-friendly and guest-worthy dinners.

Inside you'll find one hundred keto-approved recipes to help you re-create your favorite high-carb baked goods as delicious keto versions that taste amazing and are easy to replicate at home. You'll also learn keto baking basics and get a list of the best keto pantry staples for making low-carb baked goods in your own kitchen.

The recipes you'll find here are not just for breads, you'll also find items like pastry doughs, pie crusts, graham crackers, and pizza dough. You can use these recipes over and over to make things like Chicken Pot Pie, Coconut Cream Pie with Graham Cracker Crust, Classic Cheesecake (that tastes like it came straight from New York!), and even Pepperoni and Cheese Calzones. Whatever you're craving, *Keto Bread* will make it accessible to you in a way that you can still remain in ketosis. It'll feel like a "cheat," but it's not!

Keto-friendly breads and baked goods are actually important for your success on the ketogenic diet—they fill in the gap of what you're used to eating with the foods you now want to nourish your body with. By following the easy recipes and simple baking tips in these pages you can enjoy all of your favorite dishes in a low-carb way that will help you become a better, healthier you!

CHAPTER 1

INTRODUCTION TO BAKING ON THE KETO DIET

When people who choose to follow a ketogenic diet fall off the wagon, it's usually because of one of two reasons: 1) they crave bread in some form, or 2) they didn't want to feel deprived because everyone around them was eating bread. While it is true that bread is typically too high in carbohydrates to be included in the keto diet, there is hope. With a few ingredients and a little baking know-how, you won't have to give up your bread on keto!

This chapter will discuss the ketogenic diet, including what it is, the macronutrient breakdown, how to tell when your body switches over to using ketones for energy, and what to expect when your body is in ketosis. It will also go over keto baking basics and give you a list of some of the most popular keto pantry staples.

WHAT IS THE KETO DIET?

A keto diet is a low-carbohydrate, moderate-protein, high-fat diet. When you reduce your intake of carbohydrates (your body's usual source of energy), your body is forced to adapt and make ketones to use for energy instead. If you're at a caloric surplus, your body will use these ketones and fatty acid for fuel; but if you're at a caloric deficit, your body will tap into its fat storage and use your existing fat for fuel.

Let's talk about what happens in your body when you eat carbs. Carbohydrate digestion occurs in the gastrointestinal tract, starting in the mouth. First, your body breaks the carbs down into glucose, then that glucose enters the bloodstream through the small intestines, causing blood glucose (blood sugar) to rise. This rise in blood sugar triggers insulin to transport glucose from your blood into your cells so it can be used as energy. When you eat more carbohydrates than your body needs for fuel, the excess is stored as fat in the form of triglycerides.

However, when your carb intake is limited, your body must turn to alternative fuel sources. First your body will use its stored glucose (called glycogen) from the muscle and liver. After that, it will break down fat for energy, that fat coming either from your diet or stored fat in the form of fatty acids and ketones (also called ketone bodies). Even when your carb intake is limited, your body still runs on a combination of glucose, ketones, and fatty acids because your body continues to produce glucose through a process called gluconeogenesis. Because of this, carbs are not a required macronutrient for most people.

When transitioning into a ketogenic diet, the method of transition is largely based on each individual person. Some people do well going "cold turkey" and jumping right into a strict keto diet, while others need to gradually reduce their carbohydrate intake a few weeks prior to starting a ketogenic diet to be able to succeed. Additionally, a person's motivation for starting a ketogenic lifestyle plays a role. For example, if a doctor prescribes a keto diet for someone with epilepsy they may start it sooner than someone who starts a keto diet for weight loss.

WHAT IS KETOSIS?

Ketosis is the state of having elevated blood ketone levels, meaning that your body is now effectively burning fat for energy instead of carbohydrates. This can happen a few different ways:

- By following a very low-carb, high-fat diet
- By fasting (not eating or consuming drinks with calories)
- By prolonged strenuous exercise

When you are in ketosis your body produces ketones to use as fuel either from the fat you eat or from the stored fat in your body.

When you're in a state of nutritional ketosis, it's easier to tap into stored fat for fuel than if you were on a carbohydrate-based diet. This is because your blood sugar level isn't constantly being spiked due to carbohydrate intake, which leads to reduced hunger pangs and cravings. Because fat is so satiating, it's easier to eat at a caloric deficit and not feel deprived.

When your body is already running on fat for fuel, it will more readily tap into stored fat. This is because insulin isn't constantly being secreted, so fat-burning mode is left on. When eating at a caloric deficit while following a ketogenic diet, weight loss occurs. A big benefit of a ketogenic diet for weight loss is that you preserve more lean body mass and lose a higher percentage of fat than on a carbohydrate-based diet. Limiting carbohydrate intake forces your body to run on fat as your primary fuel source and puts you into a state of nutritional ketosis.

WHAT ARE MACRONUTRIENTS?

Macronutrients include carbohydrates, protein, and fats. They're called macronutrients because they're typically consumed in large quantities and are measured in grams instead of micrograms or milligrams. Fat and protein are needed in large amounts to ensure that your body runs efficiently and to preserve lean body mass. Previously carbohydrates were thought to be required, but now we know that isn't the case for most people because of gluconeogenesis. All of the foods that you eat contain at least one macronutrient. Carbohydrates and protein contain four calories (kcals) per gram, while fat contains nine calories (kcals) per gram. On a typical ketogenic diet, the macronutrient breakdown is as follows:

- 60–75 percent of calories from fat
- 15–30 percent of calories from protein
- 5–10 percent of calories from carbohydrates

SIGNS YOU'RE IN KETOSIS

During the first two weeks of being on the keto diet you may experience some symptoms that people refer to as the "keto flu." These symptoms may consist of the following:

- Headaches
- Chills
- Ashy skin tone
- Sensitivity to light and sound
- Nausea
- Dizziness
- Brain fog
- Insomnia
- Irritability
- GI issues

Some people say that the keto flu is your body's way of telling you that you're going through carbohydrate withdrawals, and in a way it is. These symptoms pass the way a normal flu would pass once your body adjusts to running on ketones, which can take anywhere from three days to two weeks.

There are a few things you can do to mitigate or speed up the symptoms of the keto flu:

- Get plenty of electrolytes, in the form of bone broth, pickle juice, and so on
- Drink lots of water
- Make sure to get enough sleep
- If your doctor approves it, take magnesium and potassium supplements
- Be patient with yourself—the brain fog will eventually go away and your productivity will increase

After you've gone through the keto flu period, the good stuff starts. Positive signs that you're in ketosis include:

- Increased energy
- Increased focus
- Decreased appetite
- Improved mood
- Decreased inflammation
- Weight loss (if eating at a caloric deficit)
- Elevated blood ketone levels (BHB)

Tools to Test for Ketones (In Breath, Urine, and Blood)

To be successful on the keto diet, you don't need to test yourself unless you're using this diet for therapeutic purposes or a doctor recommends it. For those who want to test, there are a few ways to test whether you're in a state of nutritional ketosis, and some are more accurate than others. When you first start a keto diet, you may not want to invest over $100 for a blood or breath meter, so you may opt for ketone urine test strips. These urine test strips are very inexpensive (under $10 for one hundred strips) and test for the presence of ketone bodies, specifically the ketone acetoacetate. These strips are an indicator that your body is now producing ketones, but currently your body is excreting them through the urine. This is the first sign you're on your way to becoming fat-adapted, which means your body is using fatty acids and ketones as a primary fuel source, which is the point of a ketogenic diet.

Once you have been following a keto diet for a while and are committed, you may decide to purchase a blood glucose meter and blood ketone meter. These meters measure blood levels of the ketone beta-hydroxybutyrate (BHB), along with blood glucose. The level of ketones in your blood indicates how deep a level of ketosis you're in. Ketones and glucose have an inverse relationship, meaning when ketone levels rise, blood sugar lowers. Some diseases or conditions that are treated with a ketogenic diet may require deeper states of ketosis to be therapeutic. The higher ketone levels are, the deeper the state of nutritional ketosis. Blood meters cost between $50 to $100, and are available on *Amazon*. We use the Keto-Mojo meter because at this time it's a fraction of the cost per strip of other brands. This meter is available on the *Keto-Mojo* website and on *Amazon*.

If you have a little more money to spend, some people opt for getting a breath ketone meter. A couple popular brands are Ketonix and LEVL. The Ketonix meter costs in the range of $150 to $250 and is available for purchase on their website. The LEVL meter is only available through the company's website for a monthly fee, which starts at $99 per month. These meters measure the amount of acetone in the breath, which is formed from the breakdown of acetoacetate (a by-product of fat metabolism), indicating that you're burning fat. (However, this doesn't necessarily mean that you're in ketosis. For example, after an intense workout it would show the presence of acetone in the breath because you're using fat for fuel during the workout although you may not be in ketosis.)

TIPS FOR YOUR KETO JOURNEY

Because the keto diet can be tricky and very different from the standard American diet (SAD), here are a few tips to help you succeed:

- Use keto baked goods as a tool to help satisfy your carb cravings while maintaining nutritional ketosis.

- Eat a variety of foods, focusing on low-carb, high-fat options such as grass-fed meat and dairy; free-range chicken and eggs; wild-caught seafood; seeds and nuts; low-carb fruits, such as berries, avocados, coconut, and olives; and low-carb vegetables, such as leafy greens, cruciferous and other nonstarchy vegetables.

- Choose top-quality healthy fats, such as grass-fed lard or tallow, coconut oil, avocado oil, olive oil, grass-fed butter and/or ghee.

- Eat foods high in magnesium and potassium or use supplements to make sure you're getting enough electrolytes to avoid muscle cramping. Similarly, make sure you're getting 3–5 grams of sodium per day (or follow your physician's advice on sodium intake) to keep your electrolyte levels balanced. We recommend using a high-quality sea salt like Redmond Real Salt, which is typically available on *Amazon* or in many grocery stores. Some people choose to use an electrolyte powder, such as Dr. Berg's Electrolyte Powder or Vega Sport Hydrator.

- Stay hydrated—water is the best way to do this! A good rule is to consume half your body weight in pounds in ounces of water.

- Get into a routine where you're meal planning and meal prepping to save time and money, and also to avoid having to resort to high-carb or fast food on busy days.

WHY YOU SHOULD MAKE KETO BAKED GOODS

Keto baked goods are a great tool to help you stay on track and stay in ketosis. Bread doesn't have to be off-limits on the keto diet; and once you learn the tricks of keto baking, you'll open yourself up to a variety of breads that will actually blow your mind with how close they are in flavor and texture to "regular" bread items! We've found that anything you're craving from your pre-keto days can most likely be re-created in a low-carb, high-fat version of itself. Think of keto baking as a way to nourish yourself with healthy energy sources without spiking your blood sugar levels, all while satisfying your cravings and enjoying the familiar comfort foods you love. Keto baking is a win-win.

The thing about a ketogenic diet, like any other diet where you're avoiding certain foods (here, it's carbs that are the devil...well, not really, but we tend to avoid them at all costs), is that it's a mental thing. If you tell yourself you can't have bread, you'll want bread even more. Let's give an example: Right now, don't imagine a red car. Whatever you do, don't picture a red car in your mind. You can think about baseball or a glass of milk, but just don't envision a red car! Okay, by now you're probably seeing nothing but a red car in your head. This is just the way our brains operate. If we're told that we can't do or can't have something, it's all we can think about and we want it way more than we normally would.

People just starting on a keto diet probably have in mind that bread is a no-go, no how, no way, *never*. Butter, bacon, and burgers are where it's at all the time. But no matter what, no bread, ever again! Then suddenly, even though you didn't even like bread that much to begin with, bread is now all you can think about.

If that sounds a little too familiar, this bread book will save you! We made a Sandwich Bread that slices like the real deal (and grills up to the absolute best-ever Epic Grilled Cheese). Our Naan puts bread back into Indian night (along with our Butter Chicken with Naan and Spinach Curry with Naan). We do tons of sub shop classics, like Philly Cheesesteak Hoagies, BLT on "White" Bread, Pizza Subs, The Reuben, and Chicken Bacon Ranch Sandwiches. You'll enjoy a keto-fied breakfast for dinner with our Oven-Fried Chicken and Waffles, Egg and Cheese English Muffin Sandwiches, and Biscuits with Sausage Gravy. There are also plenty of dishes to entertain with in case you want to have guests over and keep things keto; a few of our guest-worthy favorites are Herbed Brisket with Focaccia Bread, Carne Asada Tacos (the Soft Tortillas make them!), and Chicken Pot Pie. And because we aren't people who skip dessert (and we hope you aren't either), we have you covered with recipes like our Tiramisu, Pumpkin Pie, and French Silk Pie. This book will be your new best friend for turning a keto diet into a way of life, instead of just a diet.

KETO BAKING BASICS

Now that you know how useful keto baking is to help you stay on track, let's talk about baking, keto-style. Baking on a keto diet is a whole new world! There are no high-carb, gluten-filled flours to help things bind easily, such as wheat flour, cake flour, all-purpose flour, potato flour, quinoa flour, or brown rice flour. Instead, we typically use low-carb, high-fat ingredients like coconut flour, almond flour, sunflower seed flour, flaxseed meal, and other similar flours.

But what about binders and emulsifiers? In normal baking, gluten acts as a binder and creates a soft-textured product with a light crumb. However, with ketogenic baking, we don't use flour sources that contain gluten, so we have to improvise to get similar results. Psyllium husk, beef gelatin, ground flaxseeds, xanthan gum, and guar gum are commonly used in keto baking to help bind and emulsify baked goods.

And of course, keto baking doesn't use sugary items such as honey, maple syrup, brown sugar, white sugar, agave nectar, etc. We opt for sugar substitutes that won't cause a blood sugar spike, like stevia, erythritol, monk fruit, and so on. Our favorite way to sweeten keto baked goods is with a combination of stevia and erythritol, because stevia helps reduce the cooling effect of erythritol, and erythritol helps cut the bitterness of stevia. By cooling effect, we mean that erythritol can cause a cool breath feel as if you just ate a mint, but without the minty flavor.

THE KETO PANTRY

A keto pantry looks nothing like your typical pantry! There are no boxed brownie or cookie mixes; canned or dried beans; boxes of Hamburger Helper or mac and cheese; canola oil; vegetable oil; salad dressings full of carbs and highly processed oil; cookies; rice; wheat flour; sugar; crackers; or candy.

On the other hand, a typical keto pantry might include the following:

- Seeds and nuts, such as sunflower seeds, pecans, brazil nuts, macadamia nuts, walnuts, almonds, and pistachios
- Alternative flours like coconut flour, almond flour, and flaxseed meal
- Low-carb protein powders and collagen peptides
- Healthy fats, including coconut oil, avocado oil, olive oil, ghee, MCT oil, and MCT oil powder
- Nut butters, such as almond butter, coconut butter or manna, cacao butter, peanut butter, or macadamia nut butter
- Snacks, like low-sugar jerky, olives, unsweetened coconut chips, and dill pickles
- Condiments, such as mustard, low-sugar ketchup, dressings made with avocado oil, and mayo made with avocado oil
- Dried spices and herbs
- Sugar alternatives, such as stevia, erythritol, monk fruit, allulose, and so on

As you can see, these two pantries are drastically different. The former is full of highly processed, highly refined foods that are mostly high in carbs and are hyperpalatable. Basically, they're made full of sugar and chemicals to taste really good. When you eat only from the former pantry, your taste buds get accustomed to supersweet foods. It takes some time, but you can retrain your palate.

DEMYSTIFYING KETO BAKING STAPLES

Keto baking has some strange products that you may have never heard of before, so here is a brief description of some of the more common ingredients used.

Coconut Flour

Coconut flour is made from dried ground coconut meat, and nowadays is readily available at most supermarkets. Coconut flour is both gluten-free and low in carbohydrates, which makes it a popular baking choice for the low-carb, Paleo, and gluten-free communities. It's very high in fiber compared with other flours, and you'll need much less of it compared to other flours, such as all-purpose flour in traditional baking or almond flour in low-carb baking.

Coconut flour can be a little finicky to work with. Note that if you are using coconut flour alone in baked goods, your breads and baked goods may turn out a little on the drier, denser side. This is most likely due to the high fiber content of coconut flour and the fact that it absorbs a lot of liquid. Baked goods recipes that use a lot of coconut flour tend to add a lot of eggs to help lighten, moisten, and bind the recipe, and to provide structure.

Almond Flour

Almond flour comes from raw almonds that have had their skins removed. It's not to be confused with almond meal, which is made from raw almonds that still have their skin on, and is darker in color. Both almond flour and almond meal are used in keto baking.

Almond flour is naturally gluten-free and low in carbohydrates, and is often used in low-carb baking to replace traditional all-purpose flour. Almond flour is higher in fat and lower in fiber than coconut flour, and is normally used in higher amounts than coconut flour in recipes. Many keto and low-carb baking recipes call for a blend of both coconut and almond flour for the best results in terms of flavor and texture.

Keto baked goods that use almond flour often have psyllium husk powder, beef gelatin, and/or flaxseed meal added to them. This is to help provide a chewy bread-like texture and structure.

Psyllium Husk Powder

This is a finely ground powder made of psyllium husks. It is very high in fiber and contains a lot of water. Psyllium husk powder is used to add a more bread-like texture to keto baked goods because of their lack of gluten. Make sure you check the label and get psyllium husk powder instead of psyllium husks because they aren't interchangeable. Also, note that depending on what brand of psyllium husk powder you use, it may turn your baked goods purplish or grayish in color; it shouldn't affect the flavor though. We recommend using Bob's Red Mill Psyllium Fiber Powder or Viva Naturals Organic Psyllium Husk Powder, both of which are available on *Amazon* or through their respective websites.

Beef Gelatin

If you're familiar with gelatin desserts, you're already familiar with gelatin! In keto baking, beef gelatin helps achieve a chewy texture. As you'll see in the recipes in this book, a little goes a long way. Be sure to follow the recipe and dissolve the gelatin in boiling water before adding it to the batter or dough. Try grass-fed and pasture-raised beef gelatin for the most nutrition.

Flaxseed Meal

Flaxseed meal is made by grinding up flaxseeds into a fine powder. There are two standard types, brown and golden. Both work interchangeably in recipes, but if you have a recipe that is a lighter color, using the golden flaxseed meal will make your recipe look prettier instead of having dark specks throughout the finished product. Flaxseeds are a good source of fiber and provide omega-3 fatty acids in the form of alpha-linolenic acid (ALA). Ground flaxseeds are also used in vegan baking to make a vegan egg replacement.

Chia Seeds

Chia seeds can be used in baking either in their whole form or in a powdered form. To make powdered chia seeds, simply blend them in a high-speed blender until powdery. Chia seeds are great to add to recipes to absorb liquid, and to give a chewier texture to keto baked goods. They are also high in fiber and protein with 0 grams net carbs per serving, making them a great keto option.

Stevia

This keto-friendly sweetener comes from the leaves of a plant. Stevia is used as a sugar substitute, but tastes much sweeter than cane sugar; it can be up to three hundred times as sweet! Some people note that stevia can have a bitter aftertaste. There are several forms of stevia available, such as liquid (usually comes with a dropper), stevia glycerite (which is more viscous than regular liquid stevia, and even more highly concentrated), and powdered stevia. In its powdered form, stevia is commonly blended with another sweetener, such as erythritol, to reduce the bitterness. Be on the lookout for stevia blends that contain maltodextrin or dextrose, both of which contain calories and elicit an insulin and glucose response.

Erythritol

Erythritol is a newer sweetener to the market. It is very popular in keto and low-carb baking because of its very low glycemic index. Erythritol is not an artificial sweetener; rather, it's a sugar alcohol derived from corn or sugarcane. Erythritol typically comes in a granulated form like granulated sugar and a confectioners or powdered form like powdered sugar. Erythritol contains about 0.25 kcals per gram; compare that with regular sugar, which contains 4 kcals per gram. Erythritol is only about 70 percent as sweet as sugar so you will need to increase the amount when swapping it for sugar to achieve the same level of sweetness. But note, erythritol in higher quantities tends to create a cooling effect. Because of this, a lot of sweet baked goods recipes use a blend of erythritol and stevia to counteract both the cooling effect of erythritol and the bitter taste of stevia. Note that because erythritol is a sugar alcohol, some people may experience digestive issues if consumed in large amounts.

Monk Fruit

Native to China, monk fruit is another keto sweetener that's used as a sugar substitute. To make monk fruit sweetener, the fruit is dried and made into an extract, which is approximately 150 to 250 times as sweet as regular sugar. Monk fruit sweetener has no calories or carbs, and doesn't impact blood glucose levels. You can find monk fruit/erythritol blends available on the market that mimic the sweetness of regular sugar.

BAKED GOODS WITHOUT THE GUILT

Switching to a keto diet can be a challenge, especially when you're used to eating sweets and treats all the time. Fortunately, the recipes in this book will provide you with low-carb, great-tasting recipes to swap out with your old sugary ones so that you can seamlessly transition into a keto or low-carb diet. The recipes will transform your former carb-loving self into an excellent keto bread baker!

In addition to sweet treats, there are many recipes in this book you'll find yourself making on a regular basis to use in family dinners, such as Herbed Bread Crumbs. These are incredibly versatile and can be used as a breading in recipes like Chicken Parmesan or as a filler or bulking agent for dishes like Meatball Sliders on Garlic Bread Biscuits. And no, these aren't your usual pork rinds being ground up and used as bread crumbs! This recipe will walk you through the process step-by-step; first making the keto bread, and then drying the bread out, and finally processing and flavoring the bread crumbs.

The goal of this book is to teach you how to make fabulous keto breads and baked goods so that you can enjoy the keto lifestyle without feeling deprived. This book will help you stay on track with your keto goals, and provide you with the recipes and knowledge to do so.

CHAPTER 2
BREAD BASICS

SANDWICH BREAD

Even following a ketogenic diet, there's no reason you can't have a sandwich for lunch if that's your thing. When you want a deli meat sandwich, grilled cheese, or just a slice of toast, this Sandwich Bread is what you should reach for. It's incredibly versatile, slices up like a dream, and keeps well for up to a week if it's wrapped well and stored in the refrigerator.

Yields 1 (9" × 5") loaf | Serves 14

Avocado oil spray
2 cups almond flour
¾ cup coconut flour
2 tablespoons psyllium husk powder
1 teaspoon salt
2 teaspoons baking powder
2 teaspoons instant yeast
2 tablespoons warm water
2 teaspoons coconut sugar
1 tablespoon beef gelatin
3 tablespoons plus ¾ cup boiling water, divided
1 cup egg whites
2 tablespoons organic apple cider vinegar
5 drops liquid stevia
6 tablespoons ghee, melted and cooled slightly
1 teaspoon sesame seeds

Per Serving
Calories: 187 | Fat: 14 g
Protein: 7 g | Sodium: 244 mg
Fiber: 5 g | Carbohydrates: 10 g
Net Carbohydrates: 4 g | Sugar: 2 g

1 Preheat the oven to 350°F. Line the inside of a 9" × 5" loaf pan with parchment paper and lightly spray the inside with avocado oil.

2 In a large bowl, whisk together the almond flour, coconut flour, psyllium husk powder, salt, and baking powder.

3 In a small bowl, stir together the yeast, warm water, and coconut sugar and let it sit 10 minutes until foamy.

4 In a separate small bowl, stir together the beef gelatin and 3 tablespoons boiling water until fully dissolved.

5 In a medium bowl, stir together the dissolved yeast, dissolved gelatin, egg whites, vinegar, liquid stevia, and melted ghee.

6 Stir the egg white mixture into the dry ingredients, and then beat in the ¾ cup boiling water.

7 Immediately pour the dough into the prepared loaf pan and smooth out the top. Let it rest 3 minutes. Sprinkle the sesame seeds on top.

8 Bake until a wooden pick inserted in the center comes out clean, about 75–90 minutes, covering the top with foil to prevent overbrowning if necessary. The loaf is done when it sounds hollow when tapped on the bottom.

9 Turn off the oven, leave the door ajar, and let the bread cool 30 minutes in the warm oven.

10 Transfer the bread to a wire rack to finish cooling before slicing.

"WHEAT" BREAD

You'll be surprised by how much our "Wheat" Bread actually looks like bread! This loaf bakes up nice and fluffy with great flavor. Don't skip the sunflower seeds, sesame seeds, and chia seeds, as they add a little bit of texture, similar to a multigrain wheat bread.

Yields 1 (9" × 5") loaf | Serves 14

½ teaspoon instant yeast

1 tablespoon warm water

1¾ cups almond flour

4 tablespoons psyllium husk powder

2 teaspoons baking powder

2 tablespoons raw sunflower seeds, coarsely chopped

4 teaspoons sesame seeds

2 teaspoons chia seeds

1 teaspoon salt

2 large eggs

4 large egg whites

2 tablespoons apple cider vinegar

10 drops liquid stevia

6 tablespoons unsalted butter, melted and cooled slightly

½ cup boiling water

Per Serving
Calories: 169 | Fat: 14 g
Protein: 6 g | Sodium: 250 mg
Fiber: 5 g | Carbohydrates: 8 g
Net Carbohydrates: 3 g | Sugar: 1 g

1 Preheat the oven to 350°F. Line the inside of a 9" × 5" loaf pan with parchment paper.

2 In a small bowl, add the yeast and warm water and stir to combine. Let it sit until foamy, about 5–10 minutes.

3 In a large bowl, whisk together the almond flour, psyllium husk powder, baking powder, sunflower seeds, sesame seeds, chia seeds, and salt.

4 In a medium bowl, whisk together the eggs, egg whites, vinegar, liquid stevia, butter, and foamy yeast mixture.

5 Stir the egg mixture into the dry ingredients, and then stir in the boiling water.

6 Transfer the batter to the prepared loaf pan, spreading it out evenly.

7 Bake until the loaf is golden brown on the top and bottom and it sounds hollow when you tap the bottom, about 75 minutes. If the loaf starts to look too dark on top before it's done, cover the top with aluminum foil during the last 15 minutes of baking.

8 Turn off the oven, leave the foil on top (if used), and let the loaf cool for 30 minutes in the oven.

9 Remove and let it cool to room temperature before slicing.

Why Use Yeast in Keto Baking?

Before food ever touches your tongue, its aroma hits your nose. If your bread smells like bread, it's that much more likely to provide a satisfying experience! The yeast in this recipe is used to help our "Wheat" Bread smell like regular bread.

"WHITE" BREAD

For a long time we didn't think fluffy Wonder Bread–style white bread was possible to achieve with keto baking. This "White" Bread goes to show that anything is possible. Whey protein powder is key to the right texture, and yeast adds that bready aroma. It's light and fluffy and perfect for schmearing with butter.

Yields 1 (9" × 5") loaf | Serves 10

Avocado oil spray
½ teaspoon instant yeast
1 tablespoon warm water
6 large eggs
½ teaspoon cream of tartar
6 ounces cream cheese, softened slightly
2 tablespoons heavy whipping cream
1 teaspoon apple cider vinegar
5 drops liquid stevia
½ cup unflavored whey protein powder
½ tablespoon psyllium husk powder
¼ teaspoon salt
¼ teaspoon baking soda

Per Serving
Calories: 153 | Fat: 10 g
Protein: 13 g | Sodium: 203 mg
Fiber: 1 g | Carbohydrates: 3 g
Net Carbohydrates: 2 g | Sugar: 1 g

1 Preheat the oven to 300°F. Line a 9" × 5" loaf pan with parchment paper and lightly spray the inside with avocado oil.

2 In a small bowl, add the yeast and warm water and stir to combine. Set aside until it's foamy, about 5–10 minutes.

3 Separate the egg whites from the yolks, placing the whites and yolks in two separate large bowls.

4 Add the cream of tartar to the bowl with the egg whites. Use a handheld electric mixer to beat until the egg whites form stiff peaks. Set aside.

5 Add the cream cheese, cream, vinegar, liquid stevia, and foamy yeast mixture to the bowl with the egg yolks. Beat until well combined. Add the whey protein powder, psyllium husk powder, salt, and baking soda and beat until smooth.

6 Fold the egg whites into the egg yolk mixture a little at a time, being careful not to deflate the whites (a few streaks or lumps of egg whites are fine).

7 Pour the batter into the prepared loaf pan and bake 1 hour.

8 Turn off the oven and let the bread cool in the oven with the oven door closed for 30 minutes.

9 Cool completely before slicing.

How to Toast This Bread

This bread is quite different from regular bread and it doesn't toast evenly in a regular toaster! To toast this "White" Bread, we recommend broiling it until golden on each side; but stay with it, the broiler can be tricky! It's only when you walk away from it that something burns under the broiler.

CLOUD BREAD

If you want an easy keto bread that whips up fast with minimal effort, Cloud Bread is it. You can use it for fried egg sandwiches, BLT sandwiches, or just butter and jam sandwiches. Store leftover Cloud Bread layered between parchment paper in a covered container in the refrigerator up to one week.

Yields 8 cloud breads

3 large eggs
¼ teaspoon cream of tartar
3 ounces cream cheese, softened slightly
1 tablespoon heavy whipping cream
½ teaspoon apple cider vinegar
3 drops liquid stevia
¼ cup unflavored whey protein powder
¾ teaspoon psyllium husk powder
⅛ teaspoon salt
⅛ teaspoon baking powder

Per Serving
Calories: 95 | Fat: 6 g
Protein: 8 g | Sodium: 113 mg
Fiber: 0 g | Carbohydrates: 2 g
Net Carbohydrates: 1 g | Sugar: 1 g

1 Preheat the oven to 300°F. Line two large baking sheets with parchment paper or silicone liners. Make sure the oven racks are both in the bottom two thirds of the oven.

2 Separate the egg whites from the yolks, placing the whites and yolks in two separate large bowls.

3 Add the cream of tartar to the bowl with the egg whites. Use a handheld electric mixer to beat until the egg whites form stiff peaks. Set aside.

4 Add the cream cheese, cream, vinegar, and liquid stevia to the bowl with the egg yolks. Beat until well combined. Add the whey protein powder, psyllium husk powder, salt, and baking powder and beat until smooth.

5 Fold the egg whites into the egg yolk mixture a little at a time, being careful not to deflate the whites (a few streaks or lumps of egg whites are fine).

6 Spoon 3 tablespoons batter onto the center of one quadrant of the prepared baking sheet to make a circle; make three more circles in each quadrant of the tray. Repeat with remaining batter on the second prepared baking sheet.

7 Bake until the bread is golden, about 15–20 minutes, rotating the trays once halfway through.

8 Cool the bread on the trays, and then remove each with a thin metal spatula.

Why Is It Called Cloud Bread?

Cloud Bread, also called Oopsie Bread, has been around for a very long time in the low-carb community. Our version is a bit more bread-like, but it's still light and fluffy in texture. And these adorable little rounds actually look like clouds!

SEED AND NUT BREAD

This bread is reminiscent of a dense European bread—loaded with seeds and nuts, heavy for its size, and a great source of protein and nutrients. Slice this bread very thin (aim for ¼"-thick slices), and then smear it with butter and no-sugar-added jam (such as the Blackberry Chia Jam in Chapter 3!). This Seed and Nut Bread is also a beautiful addition to a cheese or charcuterie board.

Yields 1 (9" × 5") loaf | Serves 24

3 large eggs
¼ cup avocado oil
1 teaspoon psyllium husk powder
1 teaspoon apple cider vinegar
¾ teaspoon salt
5 drops liquid stevia
1½ cups raw unsalted almonds
½ cup raw unsalted pepitas
½ cup raw unsalted sunflower seeds
½ cup flaxseeds

Per Serving
Calories: 131 | Fat: 12 g
Protein: 5 g | Sodium: 83 mg
Fiber: 3 g | Carbohydrates: 4 g
Net Carbohydrates: 1 g | Sugar: 1 g

1 Preheat the oven to 325°F. Line a 9" × 5" loaf pan with parchment paper.

2 In a large bowl, whisk together the eggs, oil, psyllium husk powder, vinegar, salt, and liquid stevia.

3 Stir in the almonds, pepitas, sunflower seeds, and flaxseeds until well combined.

4 Pour the batter into the prepared loaf pan, smooth it out, and let it rest for 2 minutes.

5 Bake until the loaf is golden and feels hard to the touch, about 40 minutes.

6 Cool, and then slice into ¼"-thick slices.

What Are Pepitas?

The term *pepitas* is frequently used interchangeably with *pumpkin seeds*. However, pepitas are hull-less tender seeds that grow inside certain varieties of pumpkins. Pepitas are nutrient-rich and a delicious addition to this dense seeded bread.

SANDWICH BUNS

As much as we love a good lettuce-wrapped burger, bunless burger, or double burger stack with cheese sandwiched in the middle, sometimes we just want a classic burger on a bun! These keto buns are the perfect vehicle for burgers, and they're equally delicious made into a deli meat and cheese sandwich.

Yields 4 buns

½ teaspoon instant yeast

2 teaspoons warm water

½ cup plus 1 tablespoon almond flour

3 tablespoons coconut flour

½ tablespoon psyllium husk powder

¼ teaspoon plus ⅛ teaspoon salt

¼ teaspoon baking powder

1 teaspoon beef gelatin

1½ tablespoons plus 3 tablespoons boiling water, divided

¼ cup egg whites

½ tablespoon apple cider vinegar

3 drops liquid stevia

1½ tablespoons ghee, melted

1 teaspoon sesame seeds

Per Serving
Calories: 559 | Fat: 35 g
Protein: 41 g | Sodium: 991 mg
Fiber: 13 g | Carbohydrates: 25 g
Net Carbohydrates: 12 g | Sugar: 4 g

1 Preheat the oven to 350°F. Line a large baking sheet with parchment paper or a Silpat liner.

2 In a small bowl, add the yeast and warm water and stir to combine. Set aside until foamy, about 5–10 minutes.

3 In a large bowl, whisk together the almond flour, coconut flour, psyllium husk powder, salt, and baking powder.

4 In a small bowl, stir together the beef gelatin and 1½ tablespoons boiling water until fully dissolved.

5 In a medium bowl, stir together the dissolved beef gelatin, yeast mixture, egg whites, vinegar, and liquid stevia.

6 Add this egg white mixture, melted ghee, and 3 tablespoons boiling water to the dry ingredients in the large bowl, and beat with a handheld electric mixer until it forms a dough.

7 Let the dough rest for 5 minutes, and then divide it into four equal portions. Wet your hands with water just so they're damp and roll each dough piece into a ball. Arrange the balls on the prepared baking sheet and sprinkle the sesame seeds on top.

8 Bake until the rolls are golden on the bottom and have formed a hard outer crust, about 25–30 minutes. These buns should sound hollow when you tap their bottoms.

HOAGIE SANDWICH ROLLS

These rolls are absolutely perfect for making your favorite sandwiches! The little bit of Italian herb seasoning on top adds so much in terms of both flavor and aroma. As these bake your house will smell like bread and you'll think you walked into your favorite sub shop!

Yields 2 large hoagie rolls | Serves 4

Avocado oil spray

½ teaspoon instant yeast

1 tablespoon warm water

¾ cup plus 2 tablespoons almond flour

2 tablespoons psyllium husk powder

1 teaspoon baking powder

1 tablespoon raw sunflower seeds, coarsely chopped

2 teaspoons sesame seeds

1 teaspoon chia seeds

½ teaspoon salt

1 large egg

2 large egg whites

1 tablespoon apple cider vinegar

5 drops liquid stevia

3 tablespoons unsalted butter, melted and cooled slightly

¼ cup boiling water

1 teaspoon dried Italian herb seasoning

Per Serving
Calories: 292 | Fat: 24 g
Protein: 10 g | Sodium: 438 mg
Fiber: 8 g | Carbohydrates: 13 g
Net Carbohydrates: 5 g | Sugar: 1 g

1 Preheat the oven to 350°F. Form molds for the hoagie rolls by folding two large pieces of heavy-duty aluminum foil into U shapes about 10" long by 2" wide, and spray them with avocado oil. Place the foil molds onto a large baking tray.

2 In a small bowl, add the yeast and warm water and stir to combine. Let it sit until foamy, about 5–10 minutes.

3 In a medium bowl, whisk together the almond flour, psyllium husk powder, baking powder, sunflower seeds, sesame seeds, chia seeds, and salt and set aside.

4 In a large bowl, add the egg, egg whites, vinegar, liquid stevia, and melted butter and whisk to combine. Whisk in the dissolved yeast. Stir in the dry ingredients, and then beat in the boiling water. Let the dough rest for 3 minutes (it will thicken).

5 Lightly wet your hands with water to help prevent the dough from sticking (don't use oil, or it may cause the bread to get too dark). Divide the dough into two equal pieces and shape each into a log about 8"–9" long. Place each dough log into a foil mold.

6 Sprinkle the Italian herb seasoning on top of each hoagie roll.

7 Bake until the hoagies are golden outside and sound hollow when tapped on the bottom, about 1 hour.

8 Turn the oven off and leave the hoagies inside the oven for 10 minutes once they're done baking.

9 To toast the hoagies, turn the oven up to 425°F. Split the hoagies in half lengthwise and toast 5–10 minutes before making into your favorite submarine sandwich or hoagie.

ROSEMARY BLACK PEPPER FOCACCIA BREAD

This low-carb focaccia bread is the perfect complement to any keto-friendly Italian meal. It's perfectly seasoned and drizzled with olive oil, which soaks into the bread to give it a nice crusty texture without having to dimple it with your fingers like a regular focaccia recipe. The seasoning on this focaccia is reminiscent of breadsticks at an Italian restaurant or pizza shop!

Serves 8

Olive oil, for oiling the pan, plus additional 1 tablespoon, divided

1 teaspoon instant yeast

2 tablespoons warm water

1 cup almond flour

1 teaspoon psyllium husk powder

1 teaspoon baking powder

1½ cups shredded low-moisture part-skim mozzarella cheese

1 ounce cream cheese

1 large egg, beaten

1 teaspoon dried rosemary

½ teaspoon coarse salt

¼ teaspoon black pepper

Per Serving
Calories: 183 | Fat: 15 g
Protein: 9 g | Sodium: 358 mg
Fiber: 2 g | Carbohydrates: 5 g
Net Carbohydrates: 3 g | Sugar: 1 g

1 Preheat the oven to 400°F. Grease an 8" × 8" pan with olive oil.

2 In a small bowl, add the yeast and warm water and stir to combine. Set aside until it's foamy, about 5–10 minutes.

3 In a medium bowl, whisk together the almond flour, psyllium husk powder, and baking powder and set aside.

4 In a large microwave-safe bowl, add the mozzarella and cream cheese. Microwave for 60 seconds and then give it a stir, and continue microwaving in 20-second increments until the cheese is fully melted and combined when stirred.

5 Stir the foamy yeast mixture into the melted cheese until combined, and then stir in the beaten egg until combined. Stir in the almond flour mixture until it forms a dough.

6 Spread the dough evenly into the greased pan. Make sure it is smooth and spread to the edges.

7 Pour 1 tablespoon olive oil over the dough, spreading it out across the entire dough.

8 Sprinkle the dough with the dried rosemary, salt, and pepper.

9 Bake until it starts to turn golden brown on top, about 15–18 minutes. Cut the loaf into eight sticks and serve warm.

FLUFFY DINNER ROLLS

A great dinner roll pairs well with everything from pot roast, to beef stew, to roast chicken! Not only are these rolls nice and fluffy, but they smell like real bread thanks to the use of yeast. For garlic bread dinner rolls, melt 1 tablespoon of butter and brush it on the tops of these dinner rolls when they're hot out of the oven; sprinkle a little garlic powder and dried parsley flakes on top.

Yields 4 rolls

Avocado oil spray

½ teaspoon instant yeast

1 tablespoon warm water

3 large eggs

¼ teaspoon cream of tartar

3 ounces cream cheese, softened slightly

1 tablespoon heavy whipping cream

½ teaspoon apple cider vinegar

4 drops liquid stevia

¼ cup unflavored whey protein powder

¾ teaspoon psyllium husk powder

¼ teaspoon salt

⅛ teaspoon baking soda

Per Serving
Calories: 192 | Fat: 12 g
Protein: 17 g | Sodium: 299 mg
Fiber: 1 g | Carbohydrates: 3 g
Net Carbohydrates: 2 g | Sugar: 1 g

1 Preheat the oven to 300°F. Line four 1-cup capacity round oven-safe glass containers with parchment paper so that the paper covers the bottom and up the sides of each. Lightly spray the inside of each with avocado oil.

2 In a small bowl, add the yeast and warm water and stir to combine. Set aside until it's foamy, about 5–10 minutes.

3 Separate the egg whites from the yolks, placing the whites and yolks in two separate large bowls.

4 Add the cream of tartar to the bowl with the egg whites. Use a handheld electric mixer to beat until the egg whites form stiff peaks. Set aside.

5 Add the cream cheese, cream, vinegar, liquid stevia, and foamy yeast mixture to the bowl with the egg yolks. Beat until well combined. Add the whey protein powder, psyllium husk powder, salt, and baking soda and beat until smooth.

6 Fold the egg whites into the egg yolk mixture a little at a time, being careful not to deflate the whites (a few streaks or lumps of egg whites are fine).

7 Pour the batter into the four prepared containers. Bake until the rolls are puffed and golden, about 1 hour.

PIZZA DOUGH

No more skipping pizza night! You're going to love this Pizza Dough, which uses a couple easy tricks to get a bready texture and flavor. Psyllium husk powder gives it a bread-like feel, and yeast makes it actually smell like bread! Unlike a lot of low-carb pizza crusts, this one will actually hold its shape. And as a bonus, you can make this dough, shape it into a crust, and bake it ahead, so on a busy night all you have to do is add toppings to the crust and bake for a few minutes to melt the cheese.

Yields dough for 1 (12") pizza

1 teaspoon instant yeast
2 tablespoons warm water
1 cup almond flour
1 teaspoon psyllium husk powder
1 teaspoon baking powder
1½ cups shredded low-moisture part-skim mozzarella cheese
1 ounce cream cheese
1 large egg, lightly beaten
Avocado oil, olive oil, or ghee, for your hands

Per Recipe
Calories: 1,342 | Fat: 104 g
Protein: 74 g | Sodium: 1,697 mg
Fiber: 16 g | Carbohydrates: 42 g
Net Carbohydrates: 26 g | Sugar: 8 g

1 Preheat the oven to 425°F. If you have a clay baking stone, place it in the center of the oven to preheat.

2 In a small bowl, add the yeast and warm water and stir to combine. Set aside until foamy, about 5–10 minutes.

3 In a medium bowl, whisk together the almond flour, psyllium husk powder, and baking powder and set aside.

4 In a large microwave-safe bowl, add the mozzarella and cream cheese. Microwave for 60 seconds and then give it a stir, and continue microwaving in 20-second increments until the cheese is fully melted and combined when stirred.

5 Stir the foamy yeast mixture into the melted cheese until combined, and then stir in the beaten egg until combined. Stir in the almond flour mixture until it forms a dough.

6 Oil your hands and knead the dough a couple times until it comes together as a ball.

7 Roll the dough out between two pieces of parchment paper to a 12" circle. Poke the dough in several places with a fork.

8 Slide the dough circle onto the preheated clay baking stone and bake until it's starting to turn golden brown in spots, about 6 minutes. If using a large cookie sheet instead of a clay baking stone, cook 8 minutes.

9 At this point you can either let the pizza cool, wrap it well, and refrigerate it for up to three days or freeze it for up to three months. Or you can add your favorite toppings and make a pizza now!

ENGLISH MUFFINS

Split in half, toasted, and slathered with butter, these English Muffins are just as perfect for a snack as they are for breakfast. They don't have the nooks and crannies that a traditional English muffin has, but these do have a porous, somewhat scraggly surface that has a certain affinity for butter and jam.

Yields 4 muffins

1 tablespoon unsalted butter, at room temperature

2 large eggs

4 tablespoons half-and-half

3 drops liquid stevia

6 tablespoons almond flour

4 tablespoons milled golden flaxseed

1 teaspoon baking powder

⅛ teaspoon salt

Per Serving
Calories: 178 | Fat: 15 g
Protein: 7 g | Sodium: 287 mg
Fiber: 3 g | Carbohydrates: 5 g
Net Carbohydrates: 2 g | Sugar: 1 g

1 Preheat the oven to 350°F. Spread the butter on the inside of four (1-cup) oven-safe ramekins. Cut four pieces of parchment paper to fit inside the bottom of each ramekin, and place each parchment paper circle inside.

2 In a medium bowl, beat together the eggs, half-and-half, and liquid stevia.

3 In a small bowl, whisk together the almond flour, flaxseed, baking powder, and salt.

4 Stir the dry ingredients into the wet.

5 Divide the batter between the four prepared ramekins.

6 Bake until a wooden pick inserted into the center of a muffin comes out clean or with just a couple crumbs, about 20–22 minutes.

7 To remove the muffins, run a paring knife along the outside of each.

8 To serve, slice each English Muffin in half across, and toast if desired.

BASIC BISCUITS

Crispy outside, and light and fluffy inside, these keto biscuits are everything you could want in a biscuit! They're as easy to whip up as their carby counterparts, and they freeze well. To freeze them for up to three months, wrap each biscuit individually in parchment paper and store in a zip-top bag. When you want to eat them, thaw them at room temperature and reheat for 5 minutes in a 400°F oven.

Yields 4 biscuits

1 cup almond flour
1 teaspoon baking powder
¼ teaspoon salt
⅛ teaspoon black pepper
2 tablespoons chilled unsalted butter, diced
2 tablespoons heavy whipping cream
1 large egg
½ cup shredded sharp white Cheddar cheese

Per Serving
Calories: 312 | Fat: 28 g
Protein: 11 g | Sodium: 359 mg
Fiber: 3 g | Carbohydrates: 7 g
Net Carbohydrates: 4 g | Sugar: 1 g

1 Preheat the oven to 350°F. Line a large baking tray with a Silpat liner or parchment paper.

2 In a large bowl, use a fork to stir together the almond flour, baking powder, salt, and black pepper. Cut in the butter until it looks crumbly.

3 In a small bowl, beat together the cream and egg, and gradually incorporate that into the almond flour mixture. Stir in the Cheddar until it's incorporated into the dough.

4 Divide the dough into four equal pieces, and roll each into a ball (their shape doesn't have to be perfect).

5 Arrange the balls of dough on the prepared tray and bake until golden on the bottom, about 20 minutes.

6 Serve warm.

BAGELS

The distinguishing feature of a great bagel is a chewy interior lying inside a crusty exterior. It's much easier to achieve this texture with regular bagels that contain gluten, but keto bagels are a whole different story! This recipe uses beef gelatin to get a chewy texture, psyllium husk powder for a bready crumb, and yeast for aroma.

Yields 6 bagels

1 teaspoon instant yeast

1 teaspoon coconut sugar

2 tablespoons warm water

½ teaspoon beef gelatin

2 tablespoons boiling water

1 cup almond flour

1½ teaspoons psyllium husk powder

2 teaspoons baking powder

1½ cups shredded low-moisture part-skim mozzarella cheese

1 ounce cream cheese

1 large egg, lightly beaten

Avocado oil, olive oil, or ghee, for your hands

1 large egg, lightly beaten with 1 tablespoon water, for egg wash

1 tablespoon everything bagel seasoning

Per Serving
Calories: 244 | Fat: 18 g
Protein: 14 g | Sodium: 550 mg
Fiber: 3 g | Carbohydrates: 8 g
Net Carbohydrates: 5 g | Sugar: 2 g

1 Preheat the oven to 400°F. Line a large baking tray with a Silpat liner or parchment paper.

2 In a small bowl, add the yeast, coconut sugar, and warm water and stir. Set aside until foamy, about 5–10 minutes.

3 In a separate small bowl, mix together the beef gelatin and boiling water.

4 In a medium bowl, whisk together the almond flour, psyllium husk powder, and baking powder and set aside.

5 In a large microwave-safe bowl, add the mozzarella and cream cheese. Microwave for 60 seconds and then give it a stir, and continue microwaving in 20-second increments until the cheese is fully melted and combined when stirred.

6 Stir the yeast mixture and dissolved gelatin into the melted cheese until combined, then stir in the beaten egg. Stir in the almond flour mixture until it forms a dough.

7 Oil your hands and knead the dough a couple times until it comes together as a ball.

8 Divide the dough into six equal pieces. Roll each piece into a rope and attach the ends to make a bagel shape. The opening in the center should be about 1½" in diameter.

9 Arrange the bagels on the prepared baking tray. Lightly brush the tops with egg wash (discarding the extra), and sprinkle on the everything bagel seasoning.

10 Bake until golden on the bottom, about 12–14 minutes.

SWEET VANILLA CREAM BISCUITS

Once strawberry season rolls around each year, we can't help but crave strawberry shortcake. A dish of berries topped with freshly whipped cream is a wonderful substitute, but having the option to enjoy berries with a sweet keto biscuit is even more satisfying. These biscuits are also perfect with jam for breakfast or teatime.

Yields 4 biscuits

1 cup almond flour

3 tablespoons powdered erythritol

1 teaspoon baking powder

¼ teaspoon salt

2 tablespoons chilled unsalted butter, diced

2 ounces chilled cream cheese, diced

½ tablespoon pure vanilla extract

½ teaspoon pure almond extract

10 drops liquid stevia

1 large egg, lightly beaten

1 Preheat the oven to 350°F. Line a large baking sheet with parchment paper or a Silpat liner.

2 In a large bowl, whisk together the almond flour, powdered erythritol, baking powder, and salt. Cut in the butter with a fork until it looks crumbly, and then cut in the cream cheese until combined. Use a fork to mix in the vanilla and almond extracts, liquid stevia, and then the egg.

3 Divide the dough into four equal pieces, and roll each into a ball (their shape doesn't have to be perfect).

4 Arrange the balls of dough on the prepared sheet and bake until golden on the bottom, about 15–20 minutes.

5 Serve warm or at room temperature.

Per Serving
Calories: 282 | Fat: 26 g
Protein: 9 g | Sodium: 310 mg
Fiber: 3 g | Carbohydrates: 16 g
Net Carbohydrates: 4 g | Sugar: 2 g

ALL-PURPOSE ROLL-OUT CRUST FOR PIES

This crust is going to change your pie baking forever. It has a flaky texture with rich buttery flavor, and is great for using in both savory and sweet recipes. The trick to getting it to roll out nicely is to make sure it's well chilled, and then roll it out between two pieces of parchment paper. This recipe makes enough dough for a top or bottom crust, not a double crust.

Yields dough for 1 (9") pie plate

¾ teaspoon beef gelatin
4 teaspoons boiling water
½ teaspoon apple cider vinegar
3 drops liquid stevia
1 large egg white
1½ cups almond flour
2 tablespoons coconut flour
¼ teaspoon plus ⅛ teaspoon salt
¼ teaspoon psyllium husk powder
2 tablespoons chilled unsalted butter, diced
3 ounces chilled cream cheese, diced

Per Recipe
Calories: 963 | Fat: 87 g
Protein: 27 g | Sodium: 1,267 mg
Fiber: 12 g | Carbohydrates: 26 g
Net Carbohydrates: 14 g | Sugar: 6 g

1 In a small bowl, add the beef gelatin and boiling water and stir to dissolve. Allow to cool a few minutes until lukewarm. Whisk in the vinegar, liquid stevia, and egg white.

2 In a large bowl, whisk together the almond flour, coconut flour, salt, and psyllium husk powder.

3 Use a fork to combine the egg white mixture into the dry ingredients, and then cut in the butter and cream cheese until it forms a crumbly dough.

4 Gently press the dough together to form a disk. Wrap in plastic wrap and refrigerate until well chilled, at least 2 hours (or up to three days).

PRESS-IN SAVORY CRUST

This Press-In Savory Crust is perfect for making savory pies and quiches. The Italian herb seasoning and garlic powder give this a very savory flavor, but you can omit them both for a more basic (yet still not sweet) flavor profile.

Yields dough for 1 (7") springform pan or 1 (9") pie plate

1½ cups plus 1 tablespoon almond flour

½ teaspoon Italian herb seasoning

½ teaspoon garlic powder

½ teaspoon salt

¼ teaspoon black pepper

5 tablespoons unsalted butter, melted and cooled slightly

Per Recipe
Calories: 1,517 | Fat: 145 g
Protein: 38 g | Sodium: 1,234 mg
Fiber: 19 g | Carbohydrates: 39 g
Net Carbohydrates: 20 g | Sugar: 6 g

1 In a medium bowl, stir the almond flour, Italian herb seasoning, garlic powder, salt, and black pepper into the butter until well combined (it will be a bit crumbly).

2 Press into the bottom and up the sides of a 7" springform pan or a 9" pie plate. Use a fork to poke several holes in the bottom.

3 Use this crust to make your favorite quiche or savory pie recipe.

PRESS-IN SWEET CRUST

This is our go-to recipe for a lot of different desserts, including our Cream Cheese Mousse Tart (Chapter 7) and French Silk Pie (Chapter 7). It's much easier to make than a traditional roll-out pastry crust and every bit as delicious. This crust has a subtle sweetness, hint of cinnamon, and slight vanilla aroma with a deliciously crisp texture.

Yields dough for 1 (7") springform pan or 1 (9") pie plate

5 tablespoons unsalted butter, melted and cooled slightly

7 drops liquid stevia

¼ teaspoon pure vanilla extract

1½ cups plus 1 tablespoon almond flour

1 tablespoon powdered erythritol

¼ teaspoon ground cinnamon

¼ teaspoon salt

Per Recipe

Calories: 1,514 | Fat: 145 g
Protein: 38 g | Sodium: 653 mg
Fiber: 19 g | Carbohydrates: 50 g
Net Carbohydrates: 19 g | Sugar: 6 g

1 In a large bowl, whisk the butter, liquid stevia, and vanilla together.

2 Stir in the almond flour, powdered erythritol, cinnamon, and salt until well combined (it will be a bit crumbly).

3 Press into the bottom and up the sides of a 7" springform pan or a 9" pie plate. Use a fork to poke several holes in the bottom.

4 To pre-bake the crust, preheat the oven to 325°F. If using a 7" springform pan, bake for 22–25 minutes. If using a 9" pie plate, bake for 18–20 minutes. The crust is done when it's evenly golden.

GARLIC BREAD BISCUITS

We love making these Garlic Bread Biscuits into little meatball sliders, but they are also delicious served along with soup or salad. Our best pro tip when it comes to making these biscuits is to broil them (after they're done baking) until they're a nice golden brown on top—almost burned looking—because that's when they get a deliciously crisp exterior and the mozzarella inside becomes insanely gooey! Let a pat of butter melt on top and enjoy the bliss that ensues.

Yields 4 biscuits

1 cup almond flour
1 teaspoon baking powder
1 teaspoon garlic powder
1 teaspoon dried parsley flakes
¼ teaspoon salt
⅛ teaspoon black pepper
2 tablespoons chilled unsalted butter, diced
2 tablespoons heavy whipping cream
1 large egg
½ cup shredded sharp white Cheddar cheese
½ cup shredded low-moisture part-skim mozzarella cheese

1 Preheat the oven to 350°F. Line a large baking tray with a Silpat liner or parchment paper.

2 In a large bowl, use a fork to stir together the almond flour, baking powder, garlic powder, dried parsley flakes, salt, and black pepper. Cut in the butter until it looks crumbly.

3 In a small bowl, beat together the cream and egg, and gradually incorporate that into the almond flour mixture.

4 Stir in the Cheddar until it's incorporated into the dough, and then fold in the mozzarella.

5 Divide the dough into four equal pieces, and roll each into a ball (their shape doesn't have to be perfect).

6 Arrange the balls of dough on the prepared tray and bake until golden on the bottom, about 20 minutes.

7 Serve warm.

Per Serving
Calories: 357 | Fat: 31 g
Protein: 15 g | Sodium: 454 mg
Fiber: 3 g | Carbohydrates: 8 g
Net Carbohydrates: 5 g | Sugar: 2 g

CREPES

These Crepes are slightly sweet, rich and buttery, and full of vanilla aroma. You can play with the flavor profile by adding 1 teaspoon fresh orange zest or ½ teaspoon ground cinnamon. Fill them with any flavor of jam you like, and top them with a dollop of freshly whipped cream.

Yields 12 Crepes

1 cup egg whites
½ cup unsalted butter, melted
¼ cup avocado oil
1½ tablespoons pure vanilla extract
¼ teaspoon liquid stevia
1 cup almond flour
¼ cup coconut flour
1 tablespoon psyllium husk powder
1 teaspoon salt
1½ cups plus 2 tablespoons boiling water

1 In a large bowl, beat together all ingredients except the boiling water.

2 Add the boiling water and beat until smooth.

3 Heat a medium nonstick skillet over medium to medium-high heat.

4 Pour ¼ cup batter onto the heated skillet; the batter is thin enough that it will immediately spread out in a hot skillet.

5 Cook until the Crepe is golden, about 2–3 minutes.

6 Flip, and then cook until golden on the second side, about 1–1½ minutes more. Place the Crepe onto a plate, and repeat with the remaining batter.

Per Serving
Calories: 187 | Fat: 17 g
Protein: 5 g | Sodium: 237 mg
Fiber: 3 g | Carbohydrates: 5 g
Net Carbohydrates: 2 g | Sugar: 1 g

Why Do We Use Egg Whites Instead of Whole Eggs in This Recipe?

In order to keep these Crepes light and fluffy, we use only the egg whites in this recipe. Using whole eggs yielded a denser, darker-colored crepe. Because we eat with our eyes first, we felt it best to use only egg whites to yield crepes that were closer to the original in appearance.

SOFT TORTILLAS

This is a great all-purpose low-carb tortilla recipe! Soft and pliable, these tortillas are great for making lots of Mexican meals, such as tacos, burritos, and enchiladas. And you can use them to make a quick wrap with deli meat and cheese for weekday lunches.

Yields 10 tortillas

1 cup egg whites
¼ cup avocado oil
1 cup almond flour
¼ cup coconut flour
1 tablespoon psyllium husk powder
1 teaspoon salt
½ teaspoon onion powder
½ teaspoon garlic powder
1½ cups boiling water

Per Serving
Calories: 144 | Fat: 12 g
Protein: 5 g | Sodium: 283 mg
Fiber: 3 g | Carbohydrates: 6 g
Net Carbohydrates: 2 g | Sugar: 1 g

1 In a large bowl, beat together all ingredients except the boiling water.

2 Add the boiling water and beat until smooth.

3 Heat a medium nonstick skillet over medium to medium-high heat.

4 Pour ¼ cup batter onto the heated skillet. Using the measuring cup, quickly spread out the batter as thin as you can without breaking the tortilla, to a circle about 5"–6" in diameter.

5 Cook until the tortilla is golden, about 2–3 minutes.

6 Flip, and then cook until golden on the second side, about 1–2 minutes more. Place the tortilla on a plate, and repeat with the remaining batter.

Does the Water Really Need to Be Boiling for This Recipe?

Yes! It's very important to use boiling water in this recipe. We've found that using boiling water helps get rid of lumps and yields the best texture.

NAAN

What goes better with curry than Indian flatbread? It's the perfect vehicle for scooping up those flavorful, aromatic sauces. Naan should have a golden exterior without being crispy (because it's not cooked in oil), and a nice chewy texture. This Naan delivers in terms of both flavor and texture! We love serving it hot brushed with melted butter or ghee. If garlic naan is your thing, serve it brushed with melted garlic butter.

Yields 6 Naan

½ teaspoon instant yeast
1½ teaspoons warm water
½ cup coconut flour
1½ tablespoons psyllium husk powder
½ teaspoon baking powder
½ teaspoon salt
½ teaspoon garlic powder
1 tablespoon ghee, melted
1¼ cups boiling water

Per Serving
Calories: 65 | Fat: 3 g
Protein: 2 g | Sodium: 245 mg
Fiber: 4 g | Carbohydrates: 7 g
Net Carbohydrates: 3 g | Sugar: 1 g

1 In a small bowl, add the yeast and warm water and stir to combine. Set aside until foamy, about 5–10 minutes.

2 In a medium bowl, whisk together the coconut flour, psyllium husk powder, baking powder, salt, and garlic powder.

3 Stir the foamy yeast mixture into the dry ingredients, then stir in ghee and boiling water until it forms a dough.

4 Let the dough rest for 3 minutes, and then divide it into six equal pieces. Roll each piece into a ball, and then roll each ball out between two pieces of parchment paper to an oval about 5"–6" long and 3"–4" wide.

5 Preheat a medium nonstick skillet over medium to medium-high heat. Once hot, add a piece of dough to the dry skillet. Cook until golden on both sides, about 2 minutes on the first side and 1 minute on the second side. If your skillet is big enough, you can cook multiple naan at the same time, or heat another skillet. While cooking, adjust the heat level up or down slightly so the naan doesn't burn before it cooks through.

6 Serve hot.

BASIC QUICK BREAD

Quick bread is bread that's leavened with baking powder or baking soda instead of yeast, so it doesn't require any rise time. The beauty of our Basic Quick Bread is that it's perfect for making into sandwiches, for slathering with butter and serving alongside your favorite stew, or for toasting and spreading with jam.

Yields 1 (9" × 5") loaf | Serves 12

2 cups almond flour

½ cup golden milled flaxseed

2 tablespoons coconut flour

¾ teaspoon baking soda

¾ teaspoon salt

½ teaspoon psyllium husk powder

6 large eggs

½ cup heavy whipping cream

¼ cup water

1½ teaspoons apple cider vinegar

7 drops liquid stevia

Per Serving
Calories: 207 | Fat: 17 g
Protein: 8 g | Sodium: 217 mg
Fiber: 4 g | Carbohydrates: 7 g
Net Carbohydrates: 3 g | Sugar: 1 g

1 Preheat the oven to 350°F. Line a 9" × 5" loaf pan with parchment paper.

2 In a large bowl, whisk together the almond flour, flaxseed, coconut flour, baking soda, salt, and psyllium husk powder.

3 In a medium bowl, whisk together the eggs, cream, water, vinegar, and liquid stevia.

4 Add the wet ingredients to the dry and stir to combine, being careful not to overmix.

5 Pour the batter into the prepared loaf pan and bake until a wooden skewer inserted into the center comes out clean, about 50–60 minutes.

6 Cool completely before slicing.

One of Our Best Tips to Minimize the "Eggy" Flavor in Keto Bread

A lot of our bread recipes use a little bit of both apple cider vinegar and stevia. Through a lot of trial and error, we've discovered that this combination helps greatly reduce the eggy flavor that keto bread can often have. Don't worry, you won't be able to taste the vinegar or stevia!

BANANA NUT QUICK BREAD

We grew up eating homemade banana bread on the weekends, but regular banana bread uses high-carb bananas, not to mention a lot of flour and sugar. We came up with a keto version that has perfect bready texture and the heady aromas of banana, vanilla, and cinnamon. It will make even non-keto eaters think they're eating regular bread. This bread also makes a luscious French toast!

Yields 1 (9" × 5") loaf | Serves 12

2 cups almond flour
⅔ cup powdered erythritol
½ cup golden milled flaxseed
2 tablespoons coconut flour
2 teaspoons ground cinnamon
¾ teaspoon baking soda
¾ teaspoon salt
½ teaspoon psyllium husk powder
6 large eggs
½ cup heavy whipping cream
¼ cup water
1½ tablespoons banana extract
1 tablespoon pure vanilla extract
1½ teaspoons apple cider vinegar
¼ teaspoon stevia glycerite
¾ cup plus 2 tablespoons walnut pieces, divided

Per Serving
Calories: 272 | Fat: 23 g
Protein: 10 g | Sodium: 273 mg
Fiber: 5 g | Carbohydrates: 19 g
Net Carbohydrates: 4 g | Sugar: 2 g

1 Preheat the oven to 350°F. Line a 9" × 5" loaf pan with parchment paper.

2 In a large bowl, whisk together the almond flour, powdered erythritol, flaxseed, coconut flour, cinnamon, baking soda, salt, and psyllium husk powder.

3 In a medium bowl, whisk together the eggs, cream, water, banana extract, vanilla, vinegar, and stevia glycerite.

4 Add the wet ingredients to the dry and stir to combine, being careful not to overmix. Fold in ¾ cup walnuts.

5 Pour the batter into the prepared loaf pan and sprinkle the remaining 2 tablespoons walnuts on top.

6 Bake until a wooden skewer inserted into the center comes out clean, about 50–60 minutes.

7 Cool completely before slicing.

What Is Banana Extract?

Banana extract is made from bananas, alcohol, and water. We recommend looking for pure banana extract with no added sugar. It lends a lovely banana aroma to this quick bread recipe, and it's the secret ingredient that allows us to make a killer banana bread without all the carbs of regular banana bread!

ZUCCHINI QUICK BREAD

Zucchini bread is something most people think of as "off-limits" once they start a ketogenic lifestyle, but this recipe is proof that just about anything can be keto friendly. This bread has a moist, tender crumb and is full of warm spices and aromatic vanilla; the only thing missing are the carbs!

Yields 1 (9" × 5") loaf | Serves 12

2 cups almond flour

⅔ cup powdered erythritol

½ cup golden milled flaxseed

2 tablespoons coconut flour

2 teaspoons ground cinnamon

1 teaspoon ground nutmeg

¾ teaspoon baking soda

¾ teaspoon salt

½ teaspoon psyllium husk powder

6 large eggs

½ cup heavy whipping cream

1 tablespoon pure vanilla extract

1½ teaspoons apple cider vinegar

¼ teaspoon stevia glycerite

1 medium zucchini, shredded but not peeled

1 Preheat the oven to 350°F. Line a 9" × 5" loaf pan with parchment paper.

2 In a large bowl, whisk together the almond flour, powdered erythritol, flaxseed, coconut flour, cinnamon, nutmeg, baking soda, salt, and psyllium husk powder.

3 In a medium bowl, whisk together the eggs, cream, vanilla, vinegar, stevia glycerite, and zucchini.

4 Add the wet ingredients to the dry and stir to combine, being careful not to overmix.

5 Pour the batter into the prepared loaf pan.

6 Bake until a wooden skewer inserted into the center comes out clean, about 60 minutes.

7 Cool completely before slicing.

Per Serving
Calories: 215 | Fat: 18 g
Protein: 9 g | Sodium: 274 mg
Fiber: 4 g | Carbohydrates: 18 g
Net Carbohydrates: 3 g | Sugar: 2 g

What's the Difference Between Golden Milled Flaxseed and Golden Flaxseed Meal?

The difference between these two ingredients is in how finely they're ground. Golden flaxseed meal is generally coarser than golden milled flaxseed. Golden milled flaxseed is actually quite a fine powder very similar to all-purpose flour. We prefer milled for the superior texture it gives; however, golden flaxseed meal will also work.

PUMPKIN SPICE QUICK BREAD

This Pumpkin Spice Quick Bread will become your new favorite quick bread and give you a reason to buy a can of pumpkin purée any time of year. Just be sure you buy unsweetened pumpkin purée, which is often labeled "solid-pack pumpkin" and don't get the pumpkin pie filling, which has added sugar!

Yields 1 (9" × 5") loaf | Serves 12

2 cups almond flour
⅔ cup powdered erythritol
½ cup golden milled flaxseed
2 tablespoons coconut flour
1½ tablespoons pumpkin pie spice mix
¾ teaspoon baking soda
¾ teaspoon salt
½ teaspoon psyllium husk powder
6 large eggs
1 cup unsweetened pumpkin purée
½ cup heavy whipping cream
1 tablespoon pure vanilla extract
1½ teaspoons apple cider vinegar
¼ teaspoon stevia glycerite
7 drops liquid stevia

Per Serving
Calories: 294 | Fat: 23 g
Protein: 11 g | Sodium: 279 mg
Fiber: 8 g | Carbohydrates: 24 g
Net Carbohydrates: 5 g | Sugar: 2 g

1 Preheat the oven to 350°F. Line a 9" × 5" loaf pan with parchment paper.

2 In a large bowl, whisk together the almond flour, powdered erythritol, flaxseed, coconut flour, pumpkin pie spice mix, baking soda, salt, and psyllium husk powder.

3 In a medium bowl, whisk together the eggs, pumpkin purée, cream, vanilla, vinegar, stevia glycerite, and liquid stevia.

4 Add the wet ingredients to the dry and stir to combine, being careful not to overmix.

5 Pour the batter into the prepared loaf pan and bake until a wooden skewer inserted into the center comes out clean, about 60–75 minutes. If necessary, cover the top with foil during the last 15 minutes of baking to prevent overbrowning.

6 Cool completely before slicing.

BASIC MUFFINS

When you have an excellent basic muffin recipe, it can serve as the base for an almost endless variety of different muffin flavors. Go classic with blueberry or chocolate chips, or go wild with bacon and Cheddar or leeks and goat cheese. Note that if you decide to go with a savory flavor, reduce the granulated erythritol to 1½ tablespoons and the stevia glycerite to 2 drops.

Yields 8 muffins

1 cup almond flour

¼ cup milled golden flaxseed

¼ cup granulated erythritol

1 tablespoon coconut flour

¼ teaspoon plus ⅛ teaspoon baking soda

¼ teaspoon plus ⅛ teaspoon salt

¼ teaspoon psyllium husk powder

3 large eggs

¼ cup heavy whipping cream

¼ cup water

1½ teaspoons apple cider vinegar

1 teaspoon pure vanilla extract

⅛ teaspoon stevia glycerite

Per Serving
Calories: 157 | Fat: 13 g
Protein: 6 g | Sodium: 205 mg
Fiber: 3 g | Carbohydrates: 11 g
Net Carbohydrates: 2 g | Sugar: 1 g

1 Preheat the oven to 350°F. Line eight muffin wells in a muffin tray with paper liners.

2 In a large bowl, whisk together the almond flour, flaxseed, granulated erythritol, coconut flour, baking soda, salt, and psyllium husk powder.

3 In a medium bowl, whisk together the eggs, cream, water, vinegar, vanilla, and stevia glycerite.

4 Add the wet ingredients to the dry and stir to combine, being careful not to overmix.

5 Pour the batter into the prepared muffin wells and bake until a wooden skewer inserted into the center comes out clean, about 22–26 minutes.

CORN BREAD MUFFINS

Corn Bread Muffins are all about the flavor and the texture. These muffins have a perfectly balanced sweet and savory flavor profile, and a slightly grainy texture just like real corn bread muffins! Our secret ingredient is golden flaxseed meal, which adds the texture we're looking for here.

Yields 8 muffins

1 cup almond flour

2 tablespoons coconut flour

1 tablespoon golden flaxseed meal

1½ teaspoons baking powder

½ teaspoon salt

¼ teaspoon black pepper

¼ teaspoon onion powder

2 large eggs

¼ cup water

¼ cup heavy whipping cream

4 tablespoons unsalted butter, melted and cooled slightly

1 teaspoon apple cider vinegar

5 drops liquid stevia

Per Serving
Calories: 187 | Fat: 17 g
Protein: 5 g | Sodium: 243 mg
Fiber: 2 g | Carbohydrates: 5 g
Net Carbohydrates: 2 g | Sugar: 1 g

1 Preheat the oven to 350°F. Line eight wells of a muffin tray with paper liners.

2 In a large bowl, whisk together the almond flour, coconut flour, flaxseed meal, baking powder, salt, black pepper, and onion powder.

3 In a medium bowl, whisk together the eggs, water, cream, butter, vinegar, and liquid stevia.

4 Stir the wet ingredients into the dry, and then let the batter rest for 3 minutes (it will thicken slightly).

5 Divide the batter between the eight muffin wells.

6 Bake until the muffins are golden and a wooden pick inserted in the center comes out clean, about 20–24 minutes.

Can I Use Coconut Flour and Almond Flour Interchangeably?

Coconut and almond flours have different flavors and, even more importantly, they absorb liquid differently; therefore, they cannot be used interchangeably. In many of our keto bread and baked goods recipes we use a combination of both flours for the best flavor and texture.

BLUEBERRY MUFFINS

There's just something about Blueberry Muffins that appeals to the masses! These muffins have a pleasant smell of vanilla and lemon, which makes them truly special. We're able to keep the carbs as low as possible because we just sprinkle the blueberries on top instead of mixing them into the batter.

Yields 8 muffins

1 cup almond flour

¼ cup milled golden flaxseed

¼ cup granulated erythritol

1 tablespoon coconut flour

¼ teaspoon plus ⅛ teaspoon baking soda

¼ teaspoon plus ⅛ teaspoon salt

¼ teaspoon psyllium husk powder

3 large eggs

¼ cup heavy whipping cream

¼ cup water

1½ teaspoons apple cider vinegar

1 teaspoon pure vanilla extract

⅛ teaspoon stevia glycerite

2 teaspoons lemon zest

½ cup fresh blueberries

Per Serving
Calories: 162 | Fat: 13 g
Protein: 6 g | Sodium: 205 mg
Fiber: 3 g | Carbohydrates: 12 g
Net Carbohydrates: 3 g | Sugar: 2 g

1 Preheat the oven to 350°F. Line eight muffin wells in a muffin tray with paper liners.

2 In a large bowl, whisk together the almond flour, flaxseed, granulated erythritol, coconut flour, baking soda, salt, and psyllium husk powder.

3 In a medium bowl, whisk together the eggs, cream, water, vinegar, vanilla, stevia glycerite, and lemon zest.

4 Add the wet ingredients to the dry and stir to combine, being careful not to overmix.

5 Pour the batter into the prepared muffin wells and sprinkle the blueberries on top.

6 Bake until a wooden skewer inserted into the center comes out clean, about 22–26 minutes.

Make These Muffins Your Own

To switch up the flavor profile, instead of adding fresh blueberries, you can add ½ cup chopped fresh strawberries or ¼ cup stevia-sweetened chocolate chips. Or go for your favorite nuts or unsweetened shredded coconut!

HERBED BREAD CRUMBS

You'll love the versatility of these bread crumbs! Use them to coat meat like chicken tenders or vegetables such as breaded zucchini; add them in recipes for fillers and binders, or as a crunchy topping for casseroles and gratins. This supereasy bread crumb recipe will last for weeks stored in a covered container in the refrigerator.

Yields 1½ cups bread crumbs

½ loaf Basic Quick Bread (see recipe in this chapter), cut into ½" cubes

1 tablespoon Italian herb seasoning

½ teaspoon garlic powder

Per Serving (½ cup)
Calories: 419 | Fat: 35 g
Protein: 17 g | Sodium: 434 mg
Fiber: 8 g | Carbohydrates: 14 g
Net Carbohydrates: 6 g | Sugar: 2 g

1 Preheat the oven to 300°F.

2 Arrange the bread cubes in a single layer on a large baking tray and bake 60 minutes, tossing once halfway through. Cool to room temperature.

3 Add the bread cubes to a food processor and pulverize until they form crumbs (work in batches if your food processor is small).

4 In a medium bowl, toss the crumbs together with the Italian herb seasoning and garlic powder.

5 Store in an airtight glass container up to three weeks.

CHAPTER 3

BREAKFAST

BLACKBERRY CHIA JAM AND SWEET VANILLA CREAM BISCUITS

This jam reminds Faith of summers spent at her grandparents' house in the countryside of New York where wild blackberries grew rampant. This jam cooks in just 5 minutes, and is perfect for enjoying on our Sweet Vanilla Cream Biscuits slathered with butter.

Yields 2¼ cups jam

18 ounces fresh blackberries

4 tablespoons powdered erythritol

2 tablespoons water

⅛ teaspoon stevia glycerite

Pinch salt

2 tablespoons chia seeds

1 tablespoon fresh lemon juice

¼ teaspoon pure vanilla extract

1 batch Sweet Vanilla Cream Biscuits (Chapter 2)

1 In a medium saucepan over medium-high heat, add the blackberries, powdered erythritol, water, stevia glycerite, and salt. Cover the saucepan and cook until the berries start to release their juices, about 3–5 minutes.

2 Turn off the heat and use a fork to mash the berries a bit. Stir in the chia seeds, lemon juice, and vanilla.

3 Cool to room temperature and serve on top of the Sweet Vanilla Cream Biscuits. Store any leftover jam in an airtight container in the refrigerator up to two weeks.

Per Serving (2 tablespoons)
Calories: 300 | Fat: 26 g
Protein: 9 g | Sodium: 318 mg
Fiber: 5 g | Carbohydrates: 22 g
Net Carbohydrates: 6 g | Sugar: 3 g

BISCUITS WITH SAUSAGE GRAVY

In true Southern style, these Biscuits with Sausage Gravy are down-home comfort food at its finest. This velvety gravy is thickened with cream cheese, so there's no need for another thickener. We use mild Italian turkey sausage here, but you can go with whatever your favorite kind of sausage is.

Serves 8

½ pound mild Italian turkey sausage

4 ounces cream cheese

½ cup heavy whipping cream

½ cup chicken broth

½ teaspoon garlic powder

½ teaspoon onion powder

¼ teaspoon black pepper

⅛ teaspoon salt

1 batch Basic Biscuits (Chapter 2)

1 tablespoon fresh minced parsley, for garnish

1 In a medium saucepan over medium-high heat, add the sausage. Cook until browned, about 5 minutes, using a wooden spoon to break up the meat.

2 Add the cream cheese, cream, chicken broth, garlic powder, onion powder, black pepper, and salt. Turn the heat down to medium and bring to a simmer, whisking to incorporate the cream cheese.

3 Simmer until the sauce is thickened, about 5–10 minutes, stirring frequently.

4 Serve each Biscuit warm, split open with a ¼ cup Sausage Gravy spooned inside, topped with fresh parsley.

Per Serving
Calories: 302 | Fat: 27 g
Protein: 12 g | Sodium: 465 mg
Fiber: 2 g | Carbohydrates: 5 g
Net Carbohydrates: 4 g | Sugar: 2 g

FRENCH TOAST

There's something classic about French Toast. It's truly a special dish! Here we opted to serve it with a dusting of powdered erythritol and a sprinkle of fresh berries, but you can go the more traditional route and serve it topped with stevia-sweetened maple syrup instead.

Serves 2

1 large egg

2 tablespoons heavy cream

1 tablespoon plus 2 teaspoons powdered erythritol, divided

3 drops liquid stevia

½ teaspoon pure vanilla extract

½ teaspoon ground cinnamon

4 slices Sandwich Bread (Chapter 2)

1 tablespoon coconut oil

4 tablespoons red raspberries

1 In a medium shallow bowl, lightly beat together the egg, cream, 1 tablespoon powdered erythritol, liquid stevia, vanilla, and cinnamon. Dip each slice of bread in the egg mixture, letting it soak in.

2 Heat a large nonstick skillet over medium heat. Once hot, add the coconut oil. Once the oil is melted, add the dipped bread slices.

3 Cook until the bread is golden on both sides, about 4–5 minutes on the first side and 2–3 minutes on the second side.

4 Sift the remaining 2 teaspoons powdered erythritol on top, sprinkle on the raspberries, and serve.

Per Serving
Calories: 467 | Fat: 37 g
Protein: 17 g | Sodium: 530 mg
Fiber: 11 g | Carbohydrates: 27 g
Net Carbohydrates: 10 g | Sugar: 4 g

EGG AND CHEESE ENGLISH MUFFIN SANDWICHES

Instead of hitting up the drive-through on your way to work, whip up a batch (or two) of these Egg and Cheese English Muffin Sandwiches on the weekend. Then delicious and nutritious breakfasts will be a breeze to throw together all week long! To switch up the flavors a little, you can add breakfast sausage or bacon.

Serves 4

4 large eggs

1 tablespoon ghee

4 (1-ounce) slices Gouda cheese

¾ cup arugula

4 English Muffins (Chapter 2), split in half and toasted

⅛ teaspoon black pepper

1 In a medium skillet over medium heat, fry the eggs in the ghee any way you like. Add 1 slice Gouda on top of each fried egg.

2 Divide the arugula between four English Muffin bottoms, top each with a fried egg, a sprinkle of black pepper, and then the English Muffin top.

3 Serve immediately.

Per Serving
Calories: 379 | Fat: 31 g
Protein: 21 g | Sodium: 591 mg
Fiber: 3 g | Carbohydrates: 7 g
Net Carbohydrates: 4 g | Sugar: 2 g

PANCAKES

You can use this base pancake batter recipe to make any kind of flavored pancakes you like. Blueberry and lemon zest, orange zest and cinnamon, toasted coconut, or classic chocolate chip are all delicious add-ins. This recipe makes just two servings but is easy to double, triple, or even quadruple for a crowd!

Serves 2

6 tablespoons almond flour

4 tablespoons golden milled flaxseed

1 tablespoon granulated erythritol

1 teaspoon baking powder

⅛ teaspoon salt

2 large eggs

3 tablespoons half-and-half

1 teaspoon pure vanilla extract

7 drops liquid stevia

4 teaspoons ghee

1 In a medium bowl, whisk together the almond flour, flaxseed, granulated erythritol, baking powder, and salt. Beat in the eggs, half-and-half, vanilla, and liquid stevia. Let the batter rest for 3 minutes.

2 Preheat a large cast-iron skillet over high heat. Once hot, turn the heat down to medium to medium-high.

3 Add the ghee, and use a ¼-cup measure to pour out the pancake batter into the hot skillet (you should get four Pancakes).

4 Cook until the Pancakes are light golden on both sides, flipping once, about 2–3 minutes on the first side and 1–2 minutes on the second side.

Per Serving
Calories: 296 | Fat: 25 g
Protein: 11 g | Sodium: 419 mg
Fiber: 5 g | Carbohydrates: 14 g
Net Carbohydrates: 3 g | Sugar: 2 g

To Make Extra-Fluffy Pancakes

These Pancakes have a perfectly fluffy texture as-is, but we realize that some of you like a superlight and extra-fluffy pancake! For ethereally light and fluffy pancakes, we recommend adding 1 more egg and increasing the baking powder to 1½ teaspoons. Also, make sure your eggs are at room temperature.

WAFFLES

These low-carb Waffles are perfect for breakfast, brunch, and breakfast-for-dinner! Make a double batch and store them in the freezer for a quick meal on busy mornings. Or if you like your Waffles with a savory flair, serve these up with keto fried chicken or pulled pork.

Serves 2

Nonstick spray
6 tablespoons almond flour
4 tablespoons ground flaxseed
1 scoop (26 g) unflavored whey protein powder
1 teaspoon baking powder
1 tablespoon granulated erythritol
8 drops liquid stevia
⅛ teaspoon salt
1 teaspoon pure vanilla extract
3 large eggs
2 tablespoons heavy whipping cream

1 Plug in your waffle iron. Once heated, coat with nonstick spray.

2 In a large bowl, beat together all the ingredients until well combined, making sure there are no lumps. Alternatively, you can put all the ingredients into a blender and blend until smooth.

3 Pour half of the batter into the heated and sprayed waffle iron. The Waffle is done when it starts to steam, about 2 minutes. Carefully remove the Waffle and repeat with the remaining waffle batter.

Per Serving
Calories: 406 | Fat: 29 g
Protein: 27 g | Sodium: 470 mg
Fiber: 6 g | Carbohydrates: 17 g
Net Carbohydrates: 5 g | Sugar: 2 g

Brown Flaxseed Meal versus Golden Flaxseed Meal

You can use either brown flaxseed meal or golden flaxseed meal in this recipe. In general, brown flaxseeds have a slightly stronger flavor than golden flaxseeds, but it's barely distinguishable in this recipe. The major difference you'll notice is that brown flaxseed meal gives these Waffles a "whole wheat" look, while golden flaxseed meal lends a "white bread" look.

PULL-APART CARAMEL MONKEY BREAD

This version is every bit as decadent-tasting as the classic monkey bread. Don't skip the refrigeration time for this recipe; it's important so the dough doesn't melt together as it bakes. If you're craving even more sticky sweetness, you can drizzle on a little bit of your favorite sugar-free maple-flavored syrup. Serve this hot out of the oven for the best flavor and texture!

Serves 16

2 teaspoons instant yeast

3 tablespoons warm water

2 cups almond flour

4 tablespoons powdered erythritol

4 teaspoons baking powder

2 teaspoons psyllium husk powder

1 teaspoon ground cinnamon

¼ teaspoon salt

3 cups shredded low-moisture part-skim mozzarella cheese

2 ounces cream cheese

2 large eggs, lightly beaten

2 teaspoons vanilla bean paste

½ teaspoon almond extract

¼ teaspoon stevia glycerite

Coconut oil, for your hands

3 tablespoons unsalted butter, melted

10 tablespoons granulated monk fruit/erythritol blend

Per Serving
Calories: 190 | Fat: 15 g
Protein: 9 g | Sodium: 294 mg
Fiber: 2 g | Carbohydrates: 16 g
Net Carbohydrates: 4 g | Sugar: 1 g

1 Preheat the oven to 375°F.

2 In a small bowl, add the yeast and warm water and stir to combine. Set aside until foamy, about 5–10 minutes.

3 In a medium bowl, whisk together the almond flour, powdered erythritol, baking powder, psyllium husk powder, cinnamon, and salt. Set aside.

4 In a large microwave-safe bowl, add the mozzarella and cream cheese. Microwave for 60 seconds and then give it a stir, and continue microwaving in 20-second increments until the cheese is fully melted and combined when stirred.

5 Stir the foamy yeast mixture into the melted cheese until combined. Stir in the beaten eggs, vanilla bean paste, almond extract, and stevia glycerite until combined. Stir in the almond flour mixture until it forms a dough.

6 Oil your hands with coconut oil, and knead the dough until it comes together as a ball. Cover and refrigerate 10 minutes.

7 Divide the dough into sixteen equal pieces and roll each piece into a ball. Roll each ball in melted butter and then in the granulated monk fruit/erythritol blend to coat.

8 Arrange the coated balls of dough in a Bundt cake pan; refrigerate 15 minutes.

9 Bake 30 minutes uncovered, and then cover the Bundt pan with foil and bake until a wooden pick inserted in the center comes out clean or with just a couple crumbs, about 5–10 minutes more.

10 Carefully invert onto a platter while still hot. Serve hot.

GLAZED DOUGHNUTS

If cinnamon sugar doughnuts are your thing, get ready to have your mind blown! These Glazed Doughnuts have the mouth-watering aromas of cinnamon and vanilla, a beautiful, slightly caramelized outer "crust," and a soft and tender, almost cake-like crumb. These are great with or without the glaze. Like any dough-nut, these are best if eaten the same day they're made.

Yields 6 doughnuts

DOUGHNUTS

Coconut oil spray, for your hands and the pan

1 teaspoon instant yeast

1½ tablespoons warm water

1 cup almond flour

2 tablespoons powdered erythritol

2 teaspoons baking powder

1 teaspoon psyllium husk powder

1½ teaspoons ground cinnamon, divided

⅛ teaspoon salt

1½ cups shredded low-moisture part-skim mozzarella cheese

1 ounce cream cheese

1 large egg, lightly beaten

1 teaspoon vanilla bean paste

¼ teaspoon almond extract

⅛ teaspoon stevia glycerite

3 tablespoons granulated monk fruit/erythritol blend

2 tablespoons unsalted butter, melted

For the Doughnuts:

1 Preheat the oven to 350°F. Spray the inside of a dough-nut pan with coconut oil.

2 In a small bowl, add the yeast and warm water and stir to combine. Set aside until foamy, about 5–10 minutes.

3 In a medium bowl, whisk together the almond flour, powdered erythritol, baking powder, psyllium husk powder, ½ teaspoon cinnamon, and salt. Set aside.

4 In a large microwave-safe bowl, add the mozzarella and cream cheese. Microwave for 60 seconds and then give it a stir, and continue microwaving in 20-second increments until the cheese is fully melted and combined when stirred.

5 Stir the foamy yeast mixture into the melted cheese until combined, and then stir in the beaten egg, vanilla bean paste, almond extract, and stevia glycerite until combined. Stir in the almond flour mixture until it forms a dough.

6 Oil your hands with coconut oil, and knead the dough a couple times until it comes together as a ball. Cover the dough with a piece of plastic wrap and let it sit at room temperature for 15 minutes.

7 In a shallow bowl, stir together the granulated monk fruit/erythritol blend and remaining 1 teaspoon cinnamon to make a cinnamon sugar.

8 Divide the dough into six equal pieces and roll each piece into a ball. Roll a ball in the melted butter, and then roll it in the cinnamon sugar. Poke a hole in the center of the ball and shape it into a doughnut shape. Place the doughnut

VANILLA GLAZE
8 tablespoons powdered erythritol
1 tablespoon heavy whipping cream
2 teaspoons water
½ teaspoon pure vanilla extract
Pinch salt
3 drops almond extract

Per Serving
Calories: 273 | Fat: 22 g
Protein: 12 g | Sodium: 417 mg
Fiber: 3 g | Carbohydrates: 34 g
Net Carbohydrates: 5 g | Sugar: 2 g

into the doughnut pan. Repeat with the remaining five balls of dough.

9 Bake the doughnuts until golden and a toothpick inserted in the center comes out clean or with just a couple crumbs, about 15 minutes.

10 Let the doughnuts cool in the pan 5 minutes before removing.

For the Vanilla Glaze:

1 In a medium shallow bowl, stir together all ingredients for the glaze.

2 Dip each doughnut in the glaze, and let the glaze harden before serving.

Do I Really Need a Doughnut Pan for This Recipe?

Yes! We've tried this recipe with and without a doughnut pan, and because this dough has cheese in it, these doughnuts spread out way too much and are too flat if you don't use a doughnut pan. It's well worth the investment though; you'll want to make these doughnuts all the time!

ROASTED RED PEPPER, SPINACH, AND MUSHROOM QUICHE

Quiche is a keto brunch staple, but there's no reason to save it for special occasions only! It's a balanced meal that works great for any time of day. This version is loaded with vegetables to pack a punch of nutrition. With green spinach and red bell peppers, this quiche has a festive feel and would make a lovely Christmas breakfast.

Serves 10

1 Press-In Savory Crust (Chapter 2), pressed into a 7" springform pan

2 tablespoons unsalted butter

8 ounces button mushrooms, sliced

5 ounces baby spinach

2 large cloves garlic, minced

¼ cup chopped roasted red bell pepper

4 large eggs

½ cup heavy whipping cream

½ teaspoon salt

¼ teaspoon black pepper

1 cup shredded sharp white Cheddar cheese

Per Serving
Calories: 297 | Fat: 27 g
Protein: 10 g | Sodium: 355 mg
Fiber: 2 g | Carbohydrates: 7 g
Net Carbohydrates: 4 g | Sugar: 2 g

1 Heat the oven to 350°F. Pre-bake the Press-In Savory Crust for 5 minutes.

2 Add the butter to a large, deep skillet over medium heat. Once melted, add the mushrooms and cook until softened, about 8–10 minutes, stirring occasionally. Add the spinach and garlic and cook until the spinach is wilted and the liquid is evaporated off, about 2–3 minutes, stirring continuously. Turn off the heat, stir in the roasted red bell pepper, and cool slightly.

3 In a large bowl, whisk together the eggs, cream, salt, and black pepper. Stir in the cooled vegetable mixture and the Cheddar.

4 Pour the egg mixture into the pre-baked crust.

5 Bake until the quiche is set, about 40–50 minutes.

How to Freeze Quiche for Individual Meals

Cook the quiche as directed in this recipe, and let it cool to room temperature. Cut it into ten wedges, wrap each well in parchment paper, place in a zip-top bag, and store in the freezer for up to three months. Grab a portion out as you need it! To reheat, thaw the quiche to room temperature, and then reheat it in the microwave or in a 375°F oven until warm.

MAPLE PECAN BAKED FRENCH TOAST

Richly spiced with cinnamon and nutmeg, aromatic with vanilla, and with a nutty crunch from pecans, this Maple Pecan Baked French Toast is truly worthy of a special occasion. Because it's prepared the night before, chilled overnight, and then baked in the morning, it's perfect for a stress-free, crowd-pleasing brunch.

Serves 8

1 tablespoon unsalted butter, at room temperature

10 large egg yolks

1½ cups half-and-half

½ cup heavy whipped cream

⅓ cup granulated erythritol

20 drops liquid stevia

1 tablespoon pure vanilla extract

2 teaspoons ground cinnamon

1 teaspoon ground nutmeg

¼ teaspoon salt

4 cups cubed "White" Bread (Chapter 2)

¼ cup chopped pecans

¼ cup sugar-free maple-flavored syrup (preferably stevia-sweetened maple syrup), for serving

Per Serving

Calories: 316 | Fat: 26 g
Protein: 14 g | Sodium: 242 mg
Fiber: 1 g | Carbohydrates: 16 g
Net Carbohydrates: 5 g | Sugar: 3 g

1 Spread the butter on the inside of a 1½-quart casserole dish.

2 In a large bowl, beat the egg yolks, half-and-half, cream, granulated erythritol, liquid stevia, vanilla, cinnamon, nutmeg, and salt together. Add the bread cubes and toss gently to coat.

3 Pour the mixture into the prepared casserole dish, lightly pushing down the bread so it's mostly submerged in the liquid.

4 Cover the dish with foil and refrigerate overnight.

5 Preheat the oven to 375°F. Take the casserole dish out of the refrigerator and let it sit at room temperature for 20 minutes while the oven preheats.

6 Bake the casserole (covered with foil) for 50 minutes, and then remove the foil, sprinkle the pecans on top, and bake 5 more minutes.

7 Serve warm along with maple-flavored syrup to drizzle on top.

What If I Don't Eat Maple-Flavored Syrup?

You can forgo the syrup and instead add ¼ teaspoon ground fenugreek along with the cinnamon and nutmeg in step 2. Fenugreek is a lovely spice that has a complex caramelly, maple-like flavor and aroma. It's actually one of the ingredients in artificial maple syrup, so you won't miss out on the flavor!

BREAKFAST SAUSAGE AND LEEK BREAD PUDDING

Rich and hearty, this Breakfast Sausage and Leek Bread Pudding is perfect for any meal. Here we use Corn Bread Muffins from Chapter 2 as the "bread" in this pudding to give it a little Southern flare, but if you have leftover Sandwich Bread (Chapter 2) or "White" Bread (Chapter 2), both of those are also delicious as well.

Serves 9

6 Corn Bread Muffins (Chapter 2)

1 pound Italian turkey sausage

2 leeks, white parts only, thinly sliced

2 large cloves garlic, crushed or minced

1 teaspoon minced fresh thyme

7 large eggs

1 cup heavy whipping cream

¼ cup water

1 cup shredded Gruyère cheese

¼ teaspoon salt

¼ teaspoon black pepper

Extra-virgin olive oil spray

Per Serving
Calories: 410 | Fat: 33 g
Protein: 22 g | Sodium: 637 mg
Fiber: 2 g | Carbohydrates: 7 g
Net Carbohydrates: 5 g | Sugar: 2 g

1 Preheat the oven to 350°F. Line a large baking tray with parchment paper or a Silpat liner.

2 Cut each Corn Bread Muffin into cubes, spread the cubes out on the prepared baking tray, and bake until golden, about 20 minutes. Cool.

3 Heat a large skillet over medium-high heat. Once hot, add the sausage, leeks, and garlic and cook until the meat is browned and the liquid is evaporated, about 8 minutes, stirring occasionally. Stir in the thyme. Cool.

4 In a large bowl, whisk together the eggs, cream, water, Gruyère, salt, and black pepper. Stir in the sausage mixture, and then gently stir in the corn bread cubes.

5 Spray the inside of a 9" × 13" casserole dish with extra-virgin olive oil. Pour the egg mixture into the dish. Cover the dish with foil.

6 Bake (covered) 40 minutes, and then bake (uncovered) 10 minutes more.

7 Let the casserole sit for 10–15 minutes before serving.

8 Serve warm.

Gruyère Cheese Substitutes

Gruyère cheese is wonderful in this recipe. It has a slightly nutty, buttery flavor and it melts very well. If you can find it, it's definitely worth the splurge! If you can't find Gruyère, you could substitute with Jarlsberg, Emmental, or Swiss cheese.

OVEN-FRIED CHICKEN AND WAFFLES

Many followers of the keto diet think of chicken and waffles in a longingly nostalgic way because they believe there is no way they can eat it as part of a keto lifestyle. We're here to dispel that myth! Your favorite breakfast is back.

Serves 4

1 batch Oven-Fried Chicken Tenders (Chapter 5)

1 batch Waffles (see recipe in this chapter)

¼ cup sugar-free maple-flavored syrup (preferably stevia-sweetened maple syrup), for serving

Per Serving
Calories: 462 | Fat: 26 g
Protein: 46 g | Sodium: 432 mg
Fiber: 5 g | Carbohydrates: 14 g
Net Carbohydrates: 4 g | Sugar: 2 g

Serve half of each Waffle topped with a quarter of the chicken tenders and 1 tablespoon of syrup.

CHAPTER 4

LUNCH

PANZANELLA SALAD

The best time to make this salad is when summer tomatoes are at their peak of freshness. Look for local ripe tomatoes that are in season because they'll be the sweetest and juiciest! To bump up the healthy fats in this salad, you can add chopped avocado. To make it a full meal, serve it with grilled steak or chicken!

Serves 6

CROUTONS

2 cups Basic Quick Bread (Chapter 2), cut into ½" cubes

2 tablespoons olive oil

½ teaspoon dried Italian herb seasoning

½ teaspoon garlic powder

½ teaspoon onion powder

¼ teaspoon salt

⅛ teaspoon black pepper

SALAD

¾ pound tomatoes, chopped

½ medium English cucumber, cubed but not peeled

½ small red onion, peeled and thinly sliced

1½ tablespoons extra-virgin olive oil

1 tablespoon balsamic vinegar

⅛ teaspoon salt

⅛ teaspoon black pepper

¼ cup fresh basil leaves, torn

For the Croutons:

1 Preheat the oven to 300°F.

2 In a medium bowl, toss together all ingredients for the croutons until the bread is well coated.

3 Spread the bread out onto a large baking sheet and bake for 1 hour. Cool.

For the Salad:

1 In a large salad bowl, gently toss together all ingredients for the salad with the croutons.

2 Serve immediately.

Per Serving
Calories: 212 | Fat: 18 g
Protein: 6 g | Sodium: 277 mg
Fiber: 3 g | Carbohydrates: 9 g
Net Carbohydrates: 5 g | Sugar: 3 g

CAESAR SALAD WITH HERBED CROUTONS

You're going to love these croutons so much that we recommend making a double batch! Keep them in an airtight container in the pantry for up to two weeks or in an airtight container in the refrigerator for up to two months, and use them for topping your favorite salads and soups. They are wonderfully crispy and flavorful! Note that this Caesar dressing is quite thick (almost like a dip), so you can thin it out with a little water if you'd like.

Serves 6

CROUTONS

2 cups Basic Quick Bread (Chapter 2), cut into ½" cubes

2 tablespoons olive oil

1 teaspoon minced fresh rosemary

1 teaspoon minced fresh thyme

½ teaspoon garlic powder

½ teaspoon onion powder

¼ teaspoon salt

⅛ teaspoon black pepper

DRESSING

½ cup keto-approved mayonnaise

1 large clove garlic, crushed

1 tablespoon fresh lemon juice

½ teaspoon Worcestershire sauce

½ teaspoon anchovy paste

½ teaspoon Dijon mustard

4 tablespoons fresh-grated Parmesan cheese

SALAD

2 heads romaine lettuce, torn or chopped

2 ounces shaved Parmesan cheese

Per Serving

Calories: 374 | Fat: 34 g
Protein: 13 g | Sodium: 617 mg
Fiber: 7 g | Carbohydrates: 12 g
Net Carbohydrates: 5 g | Sugar: 3 g

For the Croutons:

1 Preheat the oven to 300°F.

2 In a medium bowl, toss together all ingredients for the croutons until the bread is well coated.

3 Spread the bread out onto a large baking sheet and bake for 1 hour. Cool.

For the Dressing:

In a small bowl, stir together all ingredients, cover, and refrigerate until serving.

For the Salad:

1 In a large bowl, gently toss together the lettuce and salad dressing until the lettuce is well coated.

2 Transfer the lettuce to a serving bowl and top with the croutons and shaved Parmesan.

3 Serve immediately.

TUNA MELTS

This classic favorite school hot lunch is just as delicious as you remember from your childhood! It literally whips up in minutes, is a hit with kids and adults, and is also budget friendly. You can play with the spices and type of cheese you use to put your own spin on it!

Serves 4

2 (5-ounce) cans tuna in water, drained

6 tablespoons keto-approved mayonnaise

½ teaspoon garlic powder

½ teaspoon onion powder

¼ teaspoon sweet paprika

4 slices Sandwich Bread (Chapter 2)

4 (1-ounce) slices Cheddar cheese

Per Serving
Calories: 452 | Fat: 37 g
Protein: 20 g | Sodium: 593 mg
Fiber: 5 g | Carbohydrates: 10 g
Net Carbohydrates: 5 g | Sugar: 2 g

1 Preheat the broiler. Line a large baking tray with foil.

2 In a medium bowl, mix together the tuna, mayonnaise, garlic powder, onion powder, and sweet paprika.

3 Arrange the bread on the prepared baking tray.

4 Divide the tuna mixture between the four bread slices, and spread the mixture out. Top each with a slice of cheese.

5 Place in oven and broil until the cheese is melted.

6 Serve warm.

FRENCH ONION SOUP AU GRATIN

This recipe uses our favorite "White" Bread (Chapter 2) to make French Onion Soup au Gratin, and if no one told you it was keto, you'd never guess just by looking at it or tasting it! To add protein to this soup, you can cook stew beef in the broth until tender before topping the soups with bread and cheese and broiling.

Serves 4

2 tablespoons unsalted butter

1 large onion, peeled, halved, and thinly sliced

1 clove garlic, minced

1½ teaspoons minced fresh thyme

4 cups beef broth

1 teaspoon Worcestershire sauce

¼ teaspoon salt

⅛ teaspoon black pepper

4 slices "White" Bread (Chapter 2), toasted under the broiler

6 ounces shredded Gruyère cheese

Per Serving
Calories: 414 | Fat: 30 g
Protein: 29 g | Sodium: 1,561 mg
Fiber: 2 g | Carbohydrates: 7 g
Net Carbohydrates: 6 g | Sugar: 3 g

1 Preheat a medium saucepan over medium to medium-high heat. Add the butter and onion and cook until the onions are golden brown, about 15 minutes, stirring occasionally. (You can add a splash of water or turn the heat down as necessary if the pan gets too hot.) Add the garlic and thyme and cook 1 minute more, stirring constantly.

2 Stir in the beef broth, Worcestershire, salt, and black pepper, then bring up to a simmer and cook 3 minutes.

3 Preheat the broiler. Ladle the soup into four broiler-safe crocks. Nestle one slice of toasted bread into each crock of soup. Sprinkle the cheese on top.

4 Broil until the cheese is melted.

5 Serve.

Expand Your Cheese Horizons

Gruyère cheese is the classic choice for French Onion Soup au Gratin because of its nutty flavor and wonderful melting ability. If you can't find it or don't like it, you could also use white Cheddar, Swiss, or provolone for slightly different flavor profiles.

TOMATO SOUP AND BISCUITS

On a chilly day, there are few foods more comforting than Tomato Soup and Biscuits. What really sets this soup apart is that we use fire-roasted crushed tomatoes, which you can easily find at just about any grocery store. They're what lets you whip up a soup in less than 30 minutes that tastes like it simmered all day!

Serves 4

2 tablespoons extra-virgin olive oil

1 small onion, peeled and diced

3 large cloves garlic, minced

2 cups canned no-salt-added fire-roasted crushed tomatoes, with juices

1¼ cups vegetable stock, chicken bone broth, or water

1½ teaspoons dried Italian herb seasoning

¼ teaspoon sea salt

⅛ teaspoon black pepper

¼ cup heavy whipping cream

1 batch Basic Biscuits (Chapter 2)

1 Heat the oil in a 3-quart saucepan over medium heat. Add the onion and garlic and cook until softened, about 5–7 minutes, stirring frequently.

2 Add the tomatoes, vegetable stock, Italian herb seasoning, salt, and black pepper, and bring up to a simmer. Cover and simmer 5 minutes.

3 Cool slightly, and then carefully purée in a blender or using an immersion blender. Return soup to pot and stir in the cream.

4 Serve the soup along with the biscuits for dipping.

Per Serving
Calories: 457 | Fat: 41 g
Protein: 13 g | Sodium: 726 mg
Fiber: 5 g | Carbohydrates: 15 g
Net Carbohydrates: 10 g | Sugar: 5 g

THE REUBEN

We use our "Wheat" Bread (Chapter 2) to make this recipe, and if you're baking a loaf specifically for this, we recommend adding 2 teaspoons caraway seeds to the bread dough before baking for the most authentic flavor.

Serves 4

QUICK RUSSIAN DRESSING

5 tablespoons keto-approved mayonnaise

2 tablespoons low-carb ketchup

½ tablespoon dill pickle relish

½ teaspoon hot sauce

¼ teaspoon Worcestershire sauce

¼ teaspoon prepared regular horseradish

⅛ teaspoon onion powder

⅛ teaspoon sweet paprika

REUBEN SANDWICHES

2 slices "Wheat" Bread (Chapter 2)

2 tablespoons unsalted butter

8 (1-ounce) slices Swiss cheese

6 ounces sliced corned beef

8 tablespoons sauerkraut, liquid drained

Per Serving
Calories: 349 | Fat: 30 g
Protein: 12 g | Sodium: 942 mg
Fiber: 2 g | Carbohydrates: 4 g
Net Carbohydrates: 2 g | Sugar: 1 g

For the Quick Russian Dressing:

In a small bowl, whisk together all ingredients and set aside.

For the Reuben Sandwiches:

1 Heat a large cast-iron skillet over medium heat.

2 Butter one side of each piece of bread.

3 Place one slice of bread butter side down in the cast-iron skillet.

4 Top each piece of bread with a smear of Quick Russian Dressing, a slice of Swiss, 1½ ounces of sliced corned beef, 2 tablespoons sauerkraut, and another slice of Swiss cheese.

5 Spread additional dressing on the nonbuttered side of each remaining piece of bread, and then place the bread slices (dressing side down, butter side up) on top of each sandwich.

6 Cook until golden brown and cheese is melted, about 3–4 minutes per side.

What's the Difference Between Russian Dressing and Thousand Island Dressing?

Both dressings commonly use mayonnaise as the base and are similar in color. However, Russian dressing is more boldly flavored, with horseradish and hot sauce. Russian dressing contains dill pickle relish, while Thousand Island calls for sweet relish. Thousand Island also frequently contains hardboiled egg and olives.

BLT ON "WHITE" BREAD

The trick to this BLT is a little sprinkling of onion powder to take it over the top! These pack really well for work lunches or maybe a picnic in the park if you're so inclined.

Serves 1

2 tablespoons keto-approved mayonnaise

2 slices "White" Bread (Chapter 2)

⅛ teaspoon onion powder

2 slices tomato

1 leaf romaine lettuce

3 slices no-sugar-added bacon, cooked until crisp

1 Spread the mayonnaise on one side of each slice of bread.

2 Sprinkle onion powder on the mayonnaise.

3 Layer the tomato, lettuce, and bacon onto one slice of bread, and top with the other piece of bread.

4 Serve.

Per Serving
Calories: 629 | Fat: 52 g
Protein: 36 g | Sodium: 993 mg
Fiber: 3 g | Carbohydrates: 8 g
Net Carbohydrates: 6 g | Sugar: 3 g

What If I Don't Eat Pork?

We recommend beef bacon over other available forms of nonpork bacon because we find it's typically less processed with fewer added ingredients. Look for sugar-free grass-fed bacon (we like the US Wellness Meats brand for this!).

EPIC GRILLED CHEESE

We took your standard grilled cheese sandwich to a whole new level! We like to serve this sandwich with our favorite sugar-free BBQ sauce for dipping. Note that this recipe makes just one serving so you can easily adjust it to feed however many you need.

Serves 1

2 tablespoons unsalted butter

2 slices Sandwich Bread (Chapter 2)

1 (1-ounce) slice pepper jack cheese

3 ounces cooked brisket, shredded or sliced

1 tablespoon pickled red onions

1 (1-ounce) slice Cheddar cheese

Per Serving
Calories: 1,053 | Fat: 87 g
Protein: 51 g | Sodium: 901 mg
Fiber: 11 g | Carbohydrates: 21 g
Net Carbohydrates: 10 g | Sugar: 4 g

1 Heat a medium cast-iron skillet over medium heat.

2 Butter one side of both pieces of bread.

3 Place one slice of bread butter side down in the skillet.

4 Top with pepper jack, brisket, onions, and Cheddar.

5 Place remaining slice of bread butter side up on top of Cheddar.

6 Cook until golden brown and cheese is melted, about 3–4 minutes per side.

PIZZA SUBS

Here we use our favorite Hoagie Sandwich Rolls (Chapter 2) to put together a fast hot lunch that will have you thinking you ordered takeout from your favorite sub shop! If pepperoni isn't your thing, go with any toppings you like. Browned Italian turkey sausage is a favorite of ours, and we also like a bit of minced red onion and green bell pepper.

Serves 4

2 Hoagie Sandwich Rolls (Chapter 2)

½ cup no-sugar-added pizza sauce

2 cups shredded mozzarella cheese

2 ounces sliced uncured or regular pepperoni

Per Serving
Calories: 540 | Fat: 43 g
Protein: 25 g | Sodium: 1,065 mg
Fiber: 8 g | Carbohydrates: 16 g
Net Carbohydrates: 8 g | Sugar: 2 g

1 Preheat the oven to 400°F. Line a large baking tray with foil.

2 Split both hoagie rolls in half lengthwise and place the hoagies (cut side up) on the prepared baking tray.

3 Spread the pizza sauce on all four cut sides of the hoagies, and then sprinkle on the mozzarella. Arrange the pepperoni slices on top.

4 Bake until the cheese is melted, about 10 minutes.

5 Serve warm.

What If I Can't Find No-Sugar-Added Pizza Sauce?

If you can't find no-sugar added pizza sauce you could also cook no-sugar-added marinara sauce on the stovetop until it thickens a bit, or use a thin smear of tomato paste instead. If you're following strict keto, be sure to check the nutrition label and ingredient list to make sure the macros fit into your eating plan!

EGG SALAD SANDWICHES

Egg Salad Sandwiches are a classic lunchtime favorite, especially served with a pickle. To keep the carbs in your pickles as low as possible, look for no-sugar-added dill pickles. Egg Salad Sandwiches can also be a teatime treat; just slice the bread thinner and beat the egg salad until it's creamy, and then cut the sandwiches into little triangles.

Serves 2

4 large hard-boiled eggs, cooled and chopped

3 tablespoons keto-approved mayonnaise

1 tablespoon minced fresh parsley

¼ teaspoon garlic powder

¼ teaspoon onion powder

¼ teaspoon paprika

⅛ teaspoon salt

⅛ teaspoon black pepper

4 slices Sandwich Bread (Chapter 2)

2 large leaves butter lettuce

1 In a medium bowl, combine the eggs, mayonnaise, parsley, garlic powder, onion powder, paprika, salt, and black pepper.

2 Spread the egg salad onto two slices of Sandwich Bread. Top each with a lettuce leaf and then another slice of bread.

3 Serve.

Per Serving
Calories: 671 | Fat: 56 g
Protein: 27 g | Sodium: 889 mg
Fiber: 11 g | Carbohydrates: 22 g
Net Carbohydrates: 10 g | Sugar: 4 g

Meal Prep This Recipe

To meal prep this recipe, simply make the egg salad up to three days ahead and store it in individual serving containers in the refrigerator. Bring it to work along with Sandwich Bread (Chapter 2), or vegetable sticks for dipping, or make your sandwich in the morning on the day you want to eat it.

TURKEY AND CHEESE SUBMARINE SANDWICHES

Who says you need to stick to an "unwich" (meat and cheese rolled up with lettuce and tomato inside) just to stay keto? These subs are better than anything you could get at your local sandwich shop and you actually get to eat the bread!

Serves 4

2 Hoagie Sandwich Rolls (Chapter 2)

8 tablespoons keto-approved mayonnaise

4 slices peeled white onion

4 slices tomato

4 leaves romaine lettuce

8 ounces no-sugar-added deli-sliced turkey breast

4 ounces provolone cheese

Per Serving
Calories: 662 | Fat: 55 g
Protein: 31 g | Sodium: 1,196 mg
Fiber: 10 g | Carbohydrates: 20 g
Net Carbohydrates: 10 g | Sugar: 4 g

1 First toast the hoagie rolls: Turn the oven up to 425°F. Split the hoagies in half lengthwise and toast 5–10 minutes.

2 Spread the mayonnaise on the inside of the hoagie rolls.

3 Layer on the onion, tomato, lettuce, turkey, and cheese.

4 Close the roll and serve.

Is Deli-Sliced Turkey Breast Keto?

You might be surprised at how much sugar a lot of turkey breast from the deli has! To keep carbs low, look for turkey breast with no added sugar, and avoid ones labeled with things like "honey-smoked" or "maple-glazed." Also, be careful of pastrami seasoning and other similar flavorings because they can frequently contain quite a bit of sugar.

CHICKEN BACON RANCH SANDWICHES

Cook up extra bacon on the weekend to save for making these sandwiches for dinner during the week! This low-carb take on a sandwich shop classic hits all the same bells and whistles as the regular version, but you can be proud that you made it entirely from scratch (even the bread!).

Serves 4

8 tablespoons full-fat ranch salad dressing

8 slices Sandwich Bread (Chapter 2)

4 slices tomato

4 leaves romaine lettuce

8 slices no-sugar-added bacon, cooked until crisp

1 batch Oven-Fried Chicken Tenders (Chapter 5)

Per Serving
Calories: 856 | Fat: 61 g
Protein: 53 g | Sodium: 1,242 mg
Fiber: 13 g | Carbohydrates: 26 g
Net Carbohydrates: 13 g | Sugar: 6 g

1 Spread the ranch dressing on one side of four pieces of bread.

2 Layer on the tomato, lettuce, bacon, and chicken tenders. Top each with another slice of bread.

3 Serve.

How to Cook Bacon in the Oven

Preheat the oven to 400°F. Line a large baking sheet with foil, and then place a wire rack on top. Arrange the bacon on the wire rack in a single layer and bake until it reaches your desired crispness, about 20 minutes (no need to flip it if you're using a wire rack).

CHAPTER 5

DINNER

OVEN-FRIED CHICKEN TENDERS

These chicken tenders are supereasy to make and are done in less than 20 minutes! Thanks to the use of our Herbed Bread Crumbs (Chapter 2), these have a deliciously savory seasoned flavor. Pair them with your favorite no-sugar-added marinara sauce or low-carb ranch dressing for dipping!

Serves 4

Avocado oil spray

⅓ cup Herbed Bread Crumbs (Chapter 2)

2 tablespoons freshly grated Parmesan cheese

2 large eggs

1 pound chicken tenders

2 teaspoons coconut flour

Per Serving
Calories: 257 | Fat: 12 g
Protein: 33 g | Sodium: 204 mg
Fiber: 2 g | Carbohydrates: 3 g
Net Carbohydrates: 2 g | Sugar: 1 g

1 Preheat the oven to 425°F. Line a large baking sheet with foil and lightly spray it with avocado oil.

2 In a medium shallow bowl, combine the Herbed Bread Crumbs and Parmesan; set aside.

3 Beat the eggs in a separate medium shallow bowl and set aside.

4 Add the chicken tenders to a large zip-top plastic bag. Sprinkle in the coconut flour, seal the bag, and toss to coat the chicken tenders.

5 Working with one chicken tender at a time, shake off the excess coconut flour, dip it in the egg (and let the excess egg drip off), and then coat it in the bread crumb mixture. Place it on the prepared baking sheet. Continue this way until all the chicken tenders are coated.

6 Lightly spray the tops of the chicken tenders with avocado oil.

7 Bake until the chicken tenders are golden and crispy and reach an internal temp of 165°F, about 12 minutes, flipping once halfway through.

If You Don't Have Keto Herbed Bread Crumbs Made…

Instead of our Herbed Bread Crumbs, you can use a mixture of the following: ⅓ cup almond meal, 2 tablespoons ground pork rinds, 2 tablespoons freshly grated Parmesan cheese, ½ teaspoon dried Italian herb seasoning, and ¼ teaspoon garlic powder.

MEATBALL SLIDERS ON GARLIC BREAD BISCUITS

With cheese baked into the biscuits and more cheese melted on top, these sliders are gooey, cheesy delicious little mini sandwiches. This recipe is great if you do batch cooking on the weekend; just make the meatballs and biscuits up to three days ahead, and then assemble and bake these sliders on the day you want to eat them.

Serves 8

1 tablespoon extra-virgin olive oil

1 pound 85% lean ground beef

1 large egg, lightly beaten

½ cup almond flour

1 teaspoon Italian herb seasoning

1 teaspoon garlic powder

1 teaspoon onion powder

½ teaspoon salt

¼ teaspoon black pepper

8 Garlic Bread Biscuits (Chapter 2)

1 cup marinara sauce, warmed

1 cup shredded mozzarella cheese

1 tablespoon minced fresh parsley, for garnish

Per Serving
Calories: 548 | Fat: 44 g
Protein: 30 g | Sodium: 875 mg
Fiber: 4 g | Carbohydrates: 12 g
Net Carbohydrates: 8 g | Sugar: 4 g

1 Preheat the oven to 400°F. Line a large baking tray with foil and drizzle on the extra-virgin olive oil.

2 In a large bowl, add the ground beef, beaten egg, almond flour, Italian herb seasoning, garlic powder, onion powder, salt, and black pepper. Use your hands to combine.

3 Divide the meat mixture into sixteen pieces, rolling each into a ball.

4 Arrange the balls on the prepared baking tray, and bake until fully cooked, about 15–18 minutes.

5 Cut each Garlic Bread Biscuit in half across. Top each biscuit bottom with 1 tablespoon marinara sauce, 2 meatballs, another 1 tablespoon marinara sauce, and then 2 tablespoons shredded mozzarella. Place these onto a large baking tray lined with foil.

6 Turn oven to broil. Broil to melt the cheese, and then sprinkle on the parsley and top each with a biscuit top.

7 Serve.

SPINACH CURRY WITH NAAN

Keto can have a somewhat bad rap about being the bacon and mayonnaise diet. While it's true that a lot of us following a keto lifestyle don't steer clear of bacon or mayonnaise, it's by no means the basis of what we eat every day! This vegetable-based curry shows that you can enjoy a variety of vegetable-heavy dishes while following a keto lifestyle.

Serves 6

1 tablespoon coarse kosher salt
5 ounces baby spinach
1 medium tomato, halved
½ medium jalapeño, seeded
2 tablespoons ghee
1 small onion, peeled and diced
4 large cloves garlic, minced
1 tablespoon peeled, grated fresh ginger
1 teaspoon salt
1 teaspoon garam masala
½ teaspoon coriander
½ teaspoon cumin
¼ teaspoon turmeric
¼ teaspoon crushed red pepper flakes
1 bay leaf
8 ounces paneer cheese, cut into ½" cubes
4 tablespoons heavy whipping cream
1 tablespoon fresh lemon juice
¼ teaspoon ground fenugreek
6 Naan (Chapter 2)

1 Fill a 5-quart pot halfway full with water and bring to a boil. Add the kosher salt and the spinach. Cook the spinach until wilted, about 2 minutes, and then drain. Lightly press down on the spinach, but don't extract all the water.

2 Add the spinach, tomato, and jalapeño to a blender and process until smooth.

3 Heat the ghee in a large, deep skillet over medium heat. Add the onion and cook until softened, about 3–5 minutes, and then add the garlic and ginger and cook 1 minute more, stirring constantly.

4 Stir in the spinach purée, salt, garam masala, coriander, cumin, turmeric, crushed red pepper flakes, and bay leaf. Bring to a simmer and cook 3 minutes, stirring frequently. Add the paneer cheese and cook 1 minute more, stirring constantly.

5 Turn off the heat and stir in the cream, lemon juice, and fenugreek. Cover the skillet and let it sit for 3 minutes.

6 Remove bay leaf and discard. Serve hot, with the Naan for dipping.

Per Serving
Calories: 281 | Fat: 21 g
Protein: 13 g | Sodium: 658 mg
Fiber: 5 g | Carbohydrates: 11 g
Net Carbohydrates: 6 g | Sugar: 3 g

PHILLY CHEESESTEAK HOAGIES

These Philly Cheesesteak Hoagies bring Philly right into your kitchen, but with real foods (you won't find any fake cheese here!) and much fewer carbs.

Serves 4

2 tablespoons avocado oil, divided

½ medium onion, peeled and thinly sliced

½ medium green bell pepper, seeded and thinly sliced

1 pound ribeye steak, very thinly sliced across the grain

¼ teaspoon salt

¼ teaspoon black pepper

4 ounces sliced provolone cheese

2 Hoagie Sandwich Rolls (Chapter 2)

8 tablespoons keto-approved mayonnaise

Per Serving
Calories: 812 | Fat: 69 g
Protein: 40 g | Sodium: 1,047 mg
Fiber: 9 g | Carbohydrates: 17 g
Net Carbohydrates: 8 g | Sugar: 2 g

1 Heat 1 tablespoon avocado oil in a large skillet over medium heat. Add the onion and green bell pepper and cook until softened but not mushy, about 8 minutes, stirring occasionally. Transfer the vegetables to a bowl and set aside.

2 Turn the heat up to high and add the remaining 1 tablespoon avocado oil to the skillet. Once the pan is hot, add the sliced steak in a thin layer so it gets as much surface area on the pan as possible. Cook the meat until browned and the liquid is evaporated, about 5 minutes, stirring occasionally.

3 Add the vegetables, salt, and black pepper to the skillet with the meat. Turn off the heat, top with the provolone, and cover the skillet for a couple minutes so the cheese can melt.

4 To toast the hoagies, turn the oven on to 425°F. Split the hoagies in half lengthwise, place them on a baking tray, and toast 5–10 minutes.

5 Spread the mayonnaise on the inside of the rolls, and then top with the cheesesteak mixture.

6 Serve warm.

Is Provolone or Mozzarella Better?

In terms of carbohydrate content, provolone and mozzarella are very similar. One ounce of whole-milk mozzarella has about 0.68 grams carbohydrates and 1 ounce of provolone has about 0.61 grams carbohydrates. When it comes to flavor, the stronger, more pungent, and more complex flavor profile of provolone is the winner for Philly Cheesesteak Hoagies!

CHICKEN PARMESAN

You won't be tempted to order takeout from your favorite Italian restaurant anymore once you make this Chicken Parmesan! It has all the same flavors and textures that the classic dish has. You can even serve it on top of spiralized zucchini to get the full "pasta dinner" effect.

Serves 4

½ tablespoon extra-virgin olive oil

1 batch Oven-Fried Chicken Tenders (see recipe in this chapter)

½ cup marinara sauce

4 ounces shredded mozzarella cheese

2 tablespoons fresh torn basil

Per Serving
Calories: 374 | Fat: 21 g
Protein: 39 g | Sodium: 526 mg
Fiber: 2 g | Carbohydrates: 6 g
Net Carbohydrates: 4 g | Sugar: 3 g

1 Preheat the oven to 400°F. Drizzle the olive oil in an 8" × 8" casserole dish.

2 Arrange the Oven-Fried Chicken Tenders in the bottom of the dish. Top with the marinara sauce and then the mozzarella.

3 Bake until the cheese is melted, about 15 minutes.

4 Tear the basil right before serving and sprinkle it on top.

5 Serve immediately.

What Is the Best Vegetable to Make Into "Noodles"?

When it comes to spiralizing vegetables, anything from onion, to cucumber, to yellow squash works well! However, zucchini will forever hold a special place in our hearts because not only is it the first veggie "noodles" we ever tried, but it's also one of the easiest to handle. To keep our "zoodles" al dente, we don't cook them! Just spiralize, and they're good to go.

NAAN BBQ CHICKEN PIZZA

This recipe works great for a leftovers night after you've made roast chicken or if you pick up a rotisserie chicken. It yields just one serving (basically a personal pizza!), so you can easily adjust the recipe as needed.

Serves 1

1 Naan (Chapter 2)
2 tablespoons low-carb barbecue sauce
¼ cup chopped, cooked chicken
1 ounce shredded Cheddar cheese
1 tablespoon minced, peeled red onion
1 tablespoon chopped fresh cilantro

Per Serving
Calories: 263 | Fat: 14 g
Protein: 19 g | Sodium: 667 mg
Fiber: 5 g | Carbohydrates: 14 g
Net Carbohydrates: 9 g | Sugar: 5 g

1 Preheat the oven to 400°F. Line a large baking tray with foil.

2 Place the Naan on the prepared baking tray. Spread on the barbecue sauce and top with the chicken, Cheddar, and red onion.

3 Bake until the pizza is warm throughout, and the cheese is melted and has started to brown in spots, about 10 minutes.

4 Sprinkle the cilantro on top and serve.

SAUSAGE, BELL PEPPER, AND ONION HOAGIES

These superstuffed Sausage, Bell Pepper, and Onion Hoagies will remind you of the summertime state fair! We go for fully cooked sausage because it browns up fast, but use whatever your favorite is. Also, we won't judge if you want to add a few slices of provolone.

Serves 4

2 Hoagie Sandwich Rolls (Chapter 2)

2 tablespoons avocado oil

12 ounces fully cooked chicken sausage, sliced into rounds

1 medium onion, peeled and thinly sliced

1 medium green bell pepper, seeded and thinly sliced

8 tablespoons keto-approved mayonnaise

Per Serving
Calories: 754 | Fat: 68 g
Protein: 23 g | Sodium: 1,153 mg
Fiber: 9 g | Carbohydrates: 19 g
Net Carbohydrates: 10 g | Sugar: 3 g

1 To toast the hoagies, turn the oven up to 425°F. Split the hoagies in half lengthwise, place them on a large baking tray, and toast 5–10 minutes.

2 In a medium-large skillet over medium heat, heat the avocado oil. Add the sausage, onion, and bell pepper, and cook until the sausage is browned and the vegetables are tender but not mushy, about 8–10 minutes, stirring occasionally.

3 Spread the mayonnaise on the inside of the toasted hoagies.

4 Spoon the sausage, onion, and bell pepper mixture onto the hoagies.

5 Serve.

Is Avocado Oil Really Made from Avocados?

Yes, avocado oil is pressed from the fleshy pulp of avocados. Look for ones labeled "cold-pressed" for the most health benefits. One of the best things about avocado oil is that it has a high smoke point, typically around 500°F!

CARNE ASADA TACOS

Move over ground beef, there's a new taco in town! These Carne Asada Tacos will change your life, or at least your regular dinner rotation. Deliciously spiced and sliced nice and thin, these tacos are a nice way to spice up Taco Tuesdays or Mexican night at your family supper.

Yields 8 tacos | Serves 4

⅓ cup avocado oil

¼ cup tamari sauce

2 tablespoons fresh lime juice

1½ tablespoons apple cider vinegar

4 cloves garlic, minced

¼ teaspoon red pepper flakes

15 drops liquid stevia

1 teaspoon cumin

1 teaspoon salt

½ teaspoon black pepper

1½ pounds skirt steak

8 Soft Tortillas (Chapter 2)

8 ounces queso fresco, crumbled

½ cup fresh cilantro leaves

1 medium lime, cut into wedges

1 In a large bag or bowl, combine the avocado oil, tamari sauce, lime juice, vinegar, garlic, red pepper flakes, liquid stevia, cumin, salt, and black pepper.

2 Place the steak into the marinade, making sure to coat completely. Refrigerate for at least 1 hour.

3 Heat a large cast-iron skillet over medium heat.

4 Add the steak to the skillet, discarding the marinade, and cook about 7–10 minutes on each side, or until it reaches your desired doneness. Use a cooking thermometer to check for desired doneness (135°F for medium-rare steak). Take the steak off the heat and allow it to rest for 5 minutes. Thinly slice the steak.

5 Assemble your tacos by placing about 3 ounces of steak onto each tortilla. Top each with queso fresco and cilantro leaves. Garnish with lime wedges.

Per Serving
Calories: 670 | Fat: 44 g
Protein: 61 g | Sodium: 997 mg
Fiber: 2 g | Carbohydrates: 7 g
Net Carbohydrates: 6 g | Sugar: 0 g

How to Make This Meal Ahead

Make the Soft Tortillas up to three days in advance and store them between parchment paper in the refrigerator. To reheat the tortillas, they need only about 30 seconds in a hot (dry) skillet. You can marinate the meat in the refrigerator up to three days before cooking it, so all you have to do on the day you want to eat this meal is cook the meat!

OVEN-FRIED CHICKEN TENDER SUBS

Serve these subs with low-carb barbecue sauce or homemade blue cheese dressing for dipping.

Serves 4

2 Hoagie Sandwich Rolls (Chapter 2)

8 tablespoons keto-approved mayonnaise

4 slices peeled white onion

4 slices tomato

4 leaves romaine lettuce

1 batch Oven-Fried Chicken Tenders (see recipe in this chapter)

4 (1-ounce) slices provolone cheese

Per Serving
Calories: 884 | Fat: 66 g
Protein: 50 g | Sodium: 1,064 mg
Fiber: 11 g | Carbohydrates: 21 g
Net Carbohydrates: 9 g | Sugar: 3 g

1 To toast the hoagies, turn the oven up to 425°F. Split the hoagies in half lengthwise, place them on a large baking tray, and toast 5–10 minutes.

2 Spread the mayonnaise on the inside of the hoagies.

3 Layer on the onion, tomato, lettuce, chicken tenders, and cheese.

4 Serve.

Can I Make These Without Hoagie Rolls?

Yes! You can make sandwiches with our "White" Bread (Chapter 2) or Sandwich Bread (Chapter 2). Or, for a lighter meal, serve these subs in lettuce leaves instead of on bread (you're still getting a bready crunch from the chicken coating!).

SLOPPY JOES ON SANDWICH BUNS

Our keto version of Sloppy Joes is a little sweet, a little spicy, completely savory, and will remind you of mom's home cooking. Try not to eat it all with a spoon; the meat is fantastic on top of our Sandwich Buns (Chapter 2)!

Serves 4

2 tablespoons olive oil

1 pound 85% lean ground beef

1 medium onion, peeled and diced

4 large cloves garlic, minced

¾ cup water

14 drops liquid stevia

3 tablespoons tomato paste

2 tablespoons red wine vinegar

2 tablespoons granulated erythritol

1 tablespoon Dijon mustard

1 tablespoon Worcestershire sauce

½ tablespoon sriracha

½ tablespoon coconut aminos

1 teaspoon cumin

¾ teaspoon chipotle chili powder

½ teaspoon salt

½ teaspoon black pepper

½ teaspoon blackstrap molasses

1 batch Sandwich Buns (Chapter 2)

1 Heat a large skillet over medium-high heat. Add the olive oil and once hot, add the beef and onion. Cook until browned, about 5–7 minutes, stirring occasionally to break up the meat.

2 Add the garlic and cook 30 seconds more, stirring constantly.

3 Stir in the water, liquid stevia, tomato paste, vinegar, granulated erythritol, Dijon, Worcestershire, sriracha, coconut aminos, cumin, chipotle chili powder, salt, black pepper, and blackstrap molasses.

4 Cover the skillet, turn the heat down to simmer, and cook 20 minutes, stirring occasionally.

5 If the sauce needs additional thickening, cook it uncovered for a few minutes, stirring frequently, until it reaches your desired consistency.

6 Serve on top of Sandwich Buns.

Per Serving
Calories: 852 | Fat: 54 g
Protein: 63 g | Sodium: 1,534 mg
Fiber: 15 g | Carbohydrates: 39 g
Net Carbohydrates: 19 g | Sugar: 8 g

SALMON BURGERS WITH SPICY SLAW

These salmon patties are a great way to get in healthy fats and vitamin D. In this recipe, we use canned salmon and enhance the flavor with spices and fresh dill. You can even make these entirely from your pantry if you use dried dill and bottled lemon juice!

Serves 4

SPICY SLAW
½ small green cabbage, shredded

½ small red onion, peeled and thinly sliced

1 small carrot, peeled and shredded

1 medium jalapeño, seeded and minced

½ cup keto-approved mayonnaise

½ tablespoon apple cider vinegar

½ tablespoon Dijon mustard

3 drops liquid stevia

¼ teaspoon salt

⅛ teaspoon black pepper

SALMON BURGERS
1 (14.75-ounce) can salmon, drained

2 large eggs

½ cup Herbed Bread Crumbs (Chapter 2)

3 tablespoons fresh lemon juice

2 tablespoons minced fresh dill

½ teaspoon garlic powder

1 teaspoon Worcestershire sauce

1 teaspoon Dijon mustard

½ teaspoon salt

¼ teaspoon red pepper flakes

⅛ teaspoon black pepper

1 tablespoon avocado oil

For the Spicy Slaw:

1 In a large bowl, add shredded cabbage, onion, carrot, and jalapeño.

2 In a small bowl, mix the mayonnaise, vinegar, Dijon, liquid stevia, salt, and black pepper.

3 Pour the dressing on top of the shredded cabbage mixture and toss to coat.

4 Refrigerate at least 1 hour before serving.

For the Salmon Burgers:

1 In a large bowl, combine the salmon, eggs, bread crumbs, lemon juice, dill, garlic powder, Worcestershire, Dijon, salt, red pepper flakes, and black pepper.

2 Stir until fully combined and form into four patties.

3 Heat the avocado oil in a large skillet. Add the patties and cook until golden, about 4 minutes per side.

4 Serve the burgers topped with the slaw.

Per Serving
Calories: 485 | Fat: 40 g
Protein: 25 g | Sodium: 795 mg
Fiber: 6 g | Carbohydrates: 14 g
Net Carbohydrates: 9 g | Sugar: 6 g

HERBED BRISKET WITH FOCACCIA BREAD

We're bringing the best of your favorite barbecue joint right to your kitchen! Fresh herbs take this recipe to the next level, although in a pinch you could use dried instead. We recommend serving this up with cauliflower "mac" and cheese or coleslaw for a full meal.

Serves 8

3 pounds brisket

2 teaspoons salt

1 teaspoon black pepper

2 tablespoons avocado oil

1½ cups beef bone broth

2 teaspoons minced fresh thyme

2 teaspoons minced fresh rosemary

1 medium onion, peeled and thinly sliced

4 cloves garlic, minced

Rosemary Black Pepper Focaccia Bread (Chapter 2), cut into 8 (1") breadsticks

Per Serving

Calories: 550 | Fat: 40 g
Protein: 41 g | Sodium: 1,068 mg
Fiber: 3 g | Carbohydrates: 8 g
Net Carbohydrates: 5 g | Sugar: 2 g

1 Preheat the oven to 300°F.

2 Pat the brisket dry and season both sides with the salt and black pepper.

3 Heat a large oven-safe roasting pan over medium-high to high heat. Once hot, add the avocado oil and then sear the brisket on both sides, about 2–4 minutes per side.

4 Leave the fatty side of the brisket facing up. Add the beef bone broth, thyme, rosemary, onion, and garlic. Cover the roasting pan with aluminum foil.

5 Cook the brisket 3 hours.

6 Remove from the oven and let it rest for 20 minutes before cutting.

7 Serve brisket on top of Rosemary Black Pepper Focaccia Bread.

Why Meat Should Rest

We know how tempting it is to dive right into a well-cooked piece of meat as soon as it comes out of the oven or off the grill! But you will be well rewarded with more tender, juicier meat if you let it rest for 20 minutes before slicing so the juices have a chance to redistribute and don't seep out.

GREEK LAMB MEATBALLS WITH NAAN

This meal will remind you of gyros from your favorite Greek diner! We like to make it into a salad platter by serving the meatballs on a bed of greens (such as baby spinach or chopped romaine lettuce), and using the quick low-carb homemade Tzatziki Sauce as a salad dressing. The Naan makes this meal as close to the real deal as possible!

Serves 4

LAMB MEATBALLS

1 tablespoon extra-virgin olive oil

1 pound ground lamb

1 large egg, lightly beaten

½ cup almond flour

1 small onion, peeled and grated

1 tablespoon fresh lemon juice

2 teaspoons minced fresh rosemary

1 teaspoon garlic powder

½ teaspoon salt

¼ teaspoon black pepper

TZATZIKI SAUCE

¼ cup sour cream

¼ cup whole-milk plain Greek yogurt

1 tablespoon fresh lemon juice

1 small clove garlic, crushed

½ teaspoon dried dill

⅛ teaspoon salt

⅛ teaspoon black pepper

4 Naan (Chapter 2)

Per Serving
Calories: 473 | Fat: 34 g
Protein: 28 g | Sodium: 708 mg
Fiber: 6 g | Carbohydrates: 16 g
Net Carbohydrates: 9 g | Sugar: 4 g

For the Lamb Meatballs:

1 Preheat the oven to 400°F. Line a large baking tray with foil and drizzle on the extra-virgin olive oil.

2 In a large bowl, add the lamb, beaten egg, almond flour, onion, lemon juice, rosemary, garlic powder, salt, and black pepper. Use your hands to combine.

3 Divide the meat mixture into sixteen pieces, rolling each into a ball.

4 Arrange the balls on the prepared baking tray, and bake until fully cooked, about 15–18 minutes.

For the Tzatziki Sauce:

1 In a small bowl, stir together all ingredients except Naan and refrigerate until serving.

2 Serve the Lamb Meatballs and Tzatziki Sauce along with the Naan.

BEEF STEW WITH FLUFFY DINNER ROLLS

Beef Stew is the epitome of comfort food on a chilly fall or winter night. Our version is loaded with vegetables, breaking all the rumors that say that the keto diet doesn't include veggies! Served with Fluffy Dinner Rolls (Chapter 2), this meal will remind you of Sunday night family dinners growing up.

Serves 10

2 tablespoons ghee

2 pounds beef chuck roast, cut into 1"–2" pieces

1 large onion, peeled and chopped

8 large cloves garlic, minced

1 cup canned no-salt-added crushed tomatoes with juices

4 cups beef broth

1 bay leaf

½ tablespoon Worcestershire sauce

1 teaspoon salt

½ teaspoon black pepper

3 large stalks celery, chopped

2 medium carrots, peeled and sliced

1 cup peeled and cubed rutabaga

1 tablespoon minced fresh rosemary

1 tablespoon beef gelatin

3 tablespoons cold water

2 tablespoons minced fresh parsley

10 Fluffy Dinner Rolls (Chapter 2)

Per Serving
Calories: 326 | Fat: 20 g
Protein: 28 g | Sodium: 766 mg
Fiber: 2 g | Carbohydrates: 7 g
Net Carbohydrates: 5 g | Sugar: 3 g

1 Add the ghee to a 5-quart pot over medium-high to high heat. Once melted, add the beef cubes in a single layer and sear on both sides, about 4 minutes, turning them over once.

2 Stir in the onion and garlic and cook 1 minute, while continuing to stir.

3 Add the canned tomatoes, beef broth, bay leaf, Worcestershire, salt, and black pepper.

4 Bring up to a boil, and then cover the pot, turn the heat down to simmer, and cook until the meat is tender, but not yet falling apart, about 60–75 minutes.

5 Stir in the celery, carrots, rutabaga, and rosemary. Keep at a simmer and cook (covered) until the vegetables are tender, about 20–25 minutes.

6 In a small bowl, add the beef gelatin and sprinkle the cold water on top. Let it sit for 2 minutes, and then mix in 1 cup hot broth from the soup. Stir this mixture into the soup.

7 Stir in the parsley. Serve with Fluffy Dinner Rolls on the side for dipping.

BUTTER CHICKEN WITH NAAN

If you're as crazy about Indian food as we are, this gem of a recipe will definitely become part of your regular meal rotation! Our velvety, aromatic Indian-spiced butter sauce is paired with marinated chicken and served with our easy Naan (Chapter 2). You'll think you're dining at your favorite upscale Indian restaurant.

Serves 4

SPICE MIX
1 tablespoon garam masala
1 teaspoon cumin
½ teaspoon coriander
½ teaspoon turmeric
¼ teaspoon black pepper
¼ teaspoon ground cinnamon
¼ teaspoon ground fenugreek

CHICKEN
1 pound boneless, skinless chicken breast, cut into 1"–2" cubes
2 teaspoons Spice Mix
½ teaspoon sea salt
2 large cloves garlic, crushed
2 tablespoons fresh lemon juice
3 tablespoons sour cream

For the Spice Mix:

In a small bowl, mix together all of the spices and set aside.

For the Chicken:

1 In a medium bowl, mix together all ingredients for the chicken. Cover and refrigerate at least 2 hours or up to two days.

2 When ready, skewer the chicken and cook on a grill until fully done (it's no longer pink in the center). You can also cook it in a 400°F oven for about 10–12 minutes. Set aside.

For the Sauce:

1 Heat the ghee in a medium-large deep-sided skillet over medium heat. Once hot, add the onion and cook until softened and starting to caramelize, about 20 minutes, stirring occasionally.

2 Stir in the garlic, ginger, and remaining Spice Mix and cook 1 minute, stirring constantly.

What Is Garam Masala?

Garam masala is an Indian spice blend that usually contains some combination of the following spices: cardamom, cumin, coriander, bay leaves, black pepper, white pepper, cinnamon, cloves, and mace. It is easy to find at Indian food markets, gourmet grocery stores, and specialty spice shops.

SAUCE

4 tablespoons ghee

1 medium yellow onion, peeled and diced

3 large cloves garlic, crushed

1" piece fresh ginger, peeled and grated

Remaining Spice Mix

½ teaspoon sea salt

¼ teaspoon crushed red pepper flakes

1½ cups chicken broth

4 tablespoons tomato paste

½ cup heavy whipping cream

FOR SERVING

2 tablespoons fresh cilantro leaves, for garnish

¼ cup peeled and sliced red onion, for garnish

4 Naan (Chapter 2)

Per Serving

Calories: 492 | Fat: 33 g
Protein: 31 g | Sodium: 902 mg
Fiber: 6 g | Carbohydrates: 17 g
Net Carbohydrates: 11 g | Sugar: 6 g

3 Stir in the salt, crushed red pepper flakes, chicken broth, and tomato paste. Bring up to a boil, and then reduce the heat to simmer and cook 10 minutes.

4 Cool slightly and then carefully purée using an immersion or regular blender. Return the sauce to the skillet.

5 Stir the cooked chicken and cream into the sauce.

6 Sprinkle the fresh cilantro and sliced red onion on top, and serve with Naan for dipping.

CRISPY BAKED WHITE FISH

Say goodbye to the boxed fish sticks of your youth! This Crispy Baked White Fish is a grown-up, elegant, and much more delicious version. Serve this recipe with asparagus or broccoli to round out the meal. We think it's even pretty enough to entertain with!

Serves 4

¼ cup coconut flour
½ teaspoon salt
¼ teaspoon black pepper
1 cup Herbed Bread Crumbs (Chapter 2)
4 (4-ounce) cod filets
¼ cup extra-virgin olive oil

Per Serving
Calories: 441 | Fat: 33 g
Protein: 27 g | Sodium: 584 mg
Fiber: 7 g | Carbohydrates: 11 g
Net Carbohydrates: 5 g | Sugar: 2 g

1 Preheat the oven to 375°F. Line a large baking tray with parchment paper or a Silpat liner.

2 In a medium shallow bowl, whisk together the coconut flour, salt, and black pepper. Place the bread crumbs in a separate medium shallow bowl.

3 Dredge each piece of fish in the coconut flour mixture, and then brush both sides of each filet with olive oil.

4 Coat the oiled filets with bread crumbs, and place the filets on the prepared baking tray.

5 Cook until the fish is opaque, flakes easily with a fork, and reaches an internal temperature of 145°F, about 12–14 minutes.

Fish Alternatives

Any type of mild-flavored white fish works well in this recipe. Haddock, grouper, or halibut also work well, so feel free to go with whatever fits into your budget and is fresh at the market. We recommend finding a good fishmonger in your area who can tell you exactly where each fish comes from!

THREE-CHEESE WHITE PIZZA

When we need a crowd-pleasing pizza for a party, this one is our go-to and it's always the first to disappear off the buffet table. We start with our Pizza Dough from Chapter 2 as the crust, top it with a Garlic Cream Sauce, and then add shredded mozzarella and Cheddar. Don't be tempted to use all mozzarella, as the Cheddar adds a bit more richness that really makes this pizza special.

Yields 1 (12") pizza | Serves 8

PIZZA

1 batch Pizza Dough (Chapter 2)

6 ounces shredded mozzarella cheese

3 ounces shredded white Cheddar cheese

2 teaspoons minced fresh parsley, for garnish

GARLIC CREAM SAUCE

2 tablespoons unsalted butter

2 large cloves garlic, crushed or minced

3 ounces cream cheese

1 tablespoon heavy whipping cream

1 teaspoon dried parsley flakes

⅛ teaspoon salt

⅛ teaspoon black pepper

Per Serving

Calories: 346 | Fat: 29 g
Protein: 17 g | Sodium: 449 mg
Fiber: 2 g | Carbohydrates: 7 g
Net Carbohydrates: 5 g | Sugar: 2 g

1 Preheat the oven to 425°F. Place a clay baking stone in the center of the oven if you have one. Prepare the Pizza Dough. If using a clay baking stone, pre-bake for 6 minutes, and if using a large baking tray, pre-bake for 8 minutes. Carefully remove the pre-baked crust.

2 Leave the oven on and leave the baking stone in the center of the oven.

3 While the dough is pre-baking, make the Garlic Cream Sauce. Heat the butter in a small skillet over medium-low heat. Once melted, add the garlic and cook 1 minute, stirring constantly. Add the cream cheese, cream, dried parsley flakes, salt, and black pepper and whisk until smooth. Turn off the heat.

4 Once the crust is pre-baked, spread the Garlic Cream Sauce on top. Sprinkle on the mozzarella and Cheddar.

5 Return the pizza to the oven and bake until the cheese is melted, about 6–8 minutes.

6 Sprinkle the parsley on top and serve.

"THE WORKS" PIZZA

This fully loaded pizza is perfect for family movie night, game night with the girls, or whenever! We added all your favorite toppings, but you'll be surprised that you don't need a ton of toppings to get remarkable flavor. Be sure to check the label of your pizza sauce and choose one with no added sugar to keep carbs down.

Yields 1 (12") pizza | Serves 8

1 batch **Pizza Dough (Chapter 2)**

¾ cup **no-sugar-added pizza sauce**

8 ounces **shredded mozzarella cheese**

½ pound **mild Italian turkey sausage, browned**

3 tablespoons **peeled, minced red onion**

3 tablespoons **minced green bell pepper**

2 tablespoons **sliced black olives, patted dry**

2 tablespoons **mild banana pepper rings, drained and patted dry**

2 **button mushrooms, thinly sliced**

1 Preheat the oven to 425°F. Place a clay baking stone in the center of the oven if you have one. Prepare the Pizza Dough. If using a clay baking stone, pre-bake for 6 minutes, and if using a large baking tray, pre-bake for 8 minutes. Carefully remove the pre-baked crust.

2 Leave the oven on and leave the baking stone in the center of the oven.

3 Once the crust is pre-baked, spread the pizza sauce on top. Sprinkle on the mozzarella. Spread the sausage, red onion, green bell pepper, black olives, banana peppers, and mushrooms on top.

4 Return the pizza to the oven and bake until the cheese is melted, about 12 minutes.

5 Slice and serve.

Per Serving
Calories: 308 | Fat: 22 g
Protein: 21 g | Sodium: 590 mg
Fiber: 2 g | Carbohydrates: 8 g
Net Carbohydrates: 5 g | Sugar: 2 g

Make It a Meat Lover's Pizza!

You can make this a meat lover's pizza too! Keep the browned sausage and add pepperoni, cubed ham, and crisped and crumbled bacon. Go with any meat you like; just be sure it's fully cooked before adding it. And avoid the temptation to overload with toppings, because the crust on the outside will burn before the cheese is melted!

ENCHILADA BAKE

If you have the Soft Tortillas from Chapter 2 pre-made, this meal comes together in about 30 minutes and is proof that not every keto meal takes forever to cook! This Enchilada Bake is weeknight friendly, kid friendly, adult friendly, and even budget friendly. Make a double batch because leftovers are great for packing for lunches throughout the week.

Serves 4

Avocado oil spray
12 ounces 85% lean ground beef
3 large cloves garlic, minced
1 tablespoon tomato paste
1 tablespoon sugar-free, salt-free taco spice seasoning
1 teaspoon salt
3 drops liquid stevia
3 ounces cream cheese
¼ cup salsa
2 tablespoons water
4 Soft Tortillas (Chapter 2)
¾ cup shredded pepper jack cheese

Per Serving
Calories: 452 | Fat: 34 g
Protein: 28 g | Sodium: 1,225 mg
Fiber: 4 g | Carbohydrates: 9 g
Net Carbohydrates: 6 g | Sugar: 3 g

1 Preheat the oven to 400°F. Lightly spray the inside of an 8" × 8" casserole dish with avocado oil.

2 Heat a large skillet over medium-high heat. Once hot, add the beef and cook until browned, about 5–7 minutes, stirring occasionally to break up the meat.

3 Add the garlic and cook 30 seconds more, stirring constantly.

4 Stir in the tomato paste, taco spice seasoning, salt, and liquid stevia and turn off the heat.

5 In a small saucepan over medium heat add the cream cheese, salsa, and water and whisk until smooth. Turn off the heat.

6 To assemble each enchilada, spoon one quarter of the meat mixture into the center of each Soft Tortilla. Roll up the tortillas and place them into the prepared casserole dish.

7 Spoon the creamy salsa sauce on top and sprinkle on the pepper jack.

8 Bake until the cheese is melted, about 10–12 minutes.

9 Serve.

Freezer-Friendly Enchilada Bake

This recipe is a great choice to keep stashed in your freezer for those busy nights when you have time only for the drive-through or to throw something pre-made into the oven! Don't bake this one before you freeze it. Wrap this casserole well and store it for up to three months. When you want to make it, let it thaw to room temperature (remember to pull it out of the freezer the night before and let it thaw in the refrigerator) and then bake it as the recipe directs.

CHEESE-BURGER MELTS

If burger joints were your thing before going keto, these Cheeseburger Melts will become part of your regular dinner rotation! Play with the cheese you use to vary the flavor profile, and serve these up with a few pickles for the full experience.

Serves 4

1 pound 85% lean ground beef
½ small onion, peeled and grated
1 tablespoon Worcestershire sauce
1½ teaspoons apple cider vinegar
1 teaspoon coconut aminos
¼ teaspoon black pepper
⅛ teaspoon salt
1 tablespoon ghee, divided
6 (1-ounce) slices Cheddar cheese, cut in half
4 tablespoons unsalted butter
8 slices Sandwich Bread (Chapter 2)

Per Serving
Calories: 880 | Fat: 69 g
Protein: 45 g | Sodium: 973 mg
Fiber: 11 g | Carbohydrates: 23 g
Net Carbohydrates: 12 g | Sugar: 4 g

1 In a large bowl, add the ground beef, onion, Worcestershire, vinegar, coconut aminos, black pepper, and salt and use your hands to combine.

2 Divide the meat into eight equal pieces, roll each into a ball, and flatten to a rectangle about 4½" long by 3" wide.

3 In a large cast-iron skillet over medium-high heat, heat ½ tablespoon ghee. Once melted, add four patties and cook until browned on both sides, about 1–1½ minutes per side, flipping once halfway through. Top each patty with ½ slice of cheese and transfer the cooked patties to a plate.

4 Add the remaining ½ tablespoon ghee to the skillet and cook the remaining four patties the same way.

5 Butter one side of each piece of bread.

6 Place one slice of bread butter side down in the skillet.

7 Top with one patty (cheese facing down), ½ slice Cheddar, and one more patty (cheese facing up).

8 Place remaining slices of bread butter side up on top of each.

9 Cook sandwiches until golden brown, about 3–4 minutes per side.

How to Flavor the Best Burgers

A truly great burger is one that's juicy and flavorful, where all the seasonings just help accentuate the flavor of the meat. To achieve that, we use a few savory ingredients: onion, Worcestershire sauce, apple cider vinegar, coconut aminos (similar to soy sauce or tamari sauce), black pepper, and salt. It's a tall claim, but we think the flavor of these burgers will be the best you've ever had! If you're pressed for time, just use 1 teaspoon Montreal steak seasoning instead.

CHICKEN POT PIE

Chicken and vegetables in a rich, creamy savory sauce with a flaky pie crust on top: dinner doesn't get any better. Leftover chicken, rotisserie chicken, or even leftover turkey all work great in this recipe. You can make this filling up to two days ahead, but when you want to bake the pie, reheat the filling to a gentle simmer with an additional ¼ cup heavy whipping cream (which will change the nutrition information) before continuing on with the recipe.

Yields 1 (9") pie | Serves 8

2 tablespoons unsalted butter
2 large stalks celery, sliced
1 large carrot, peeled and sliced
1 medium onion, peeled and chopped
3 large cloves garlic, minced
1½ teaspoons minced fresh thyme
1 cup chicken broth
¼ teaspoon salt
¼ teaspoon black pepper
3 cups chopped, cooked chicken
1 ounce cream cheese
½ cup heavy whipping cream
2 tablespoons minced fresh parsley
1 batch All-Purpose Roll-Out Crust for Pies (Chapter 2), chilled
1 large egg
1 tablespoon water

Per Serving
Calories: 311 | Fat: 22 g
Protein: 21 g | Sodium: 410 mg
Fiber: 2 g | Carbohydrates: 7 g
Net Carbohydrates: 5 g | Sugar: 3 g

1 Preheat the oven to 350°F. Line a large baking tray with foil in case the pie filling bubbles up as it cooks.

2 Add the butter to a large deep skillet over medium heat. Once melted, add the celery, carrot, and onion and cook until the vegetables are starting to soften and the onion is turning translucent, about 6–8 minutes, stirring occasionally.

3 Stir in the garlic and thyme and cook until fragrant, about 1–2 minutes more.

4 Add the chicken broth, salt, and black pepper. Bring up to a boil, and then cover the skillet, turn the heat down to simmer, and cook until the vegetables are fork-tender, about 6–8 minutes.

5 Stir in the chicken, cream cheese, and cream, and bring up to a simmer. Turn off the heat and stir in the parsley.

6 Pour the pot pie filling into a 9" pie plate.

7 While it's still chilled, roll out the dough between two sheets of parchment paper to a circle about 10" in diameter.

8 Remove the top sheet of parchment paper from the dough, and pick up the bottom sheet of parchment that the rolled out dough is on. Gently flip the dough over on top of the pie, and tuck in any dough that hangs over the sides.

9 In a small bowl, whisk together the egg and water, and lightly brush the egg wash on top of the pie (discard the extra egg wash). Cut four slits in the top of the crust so steam can escape.

10 Place the pie onto the prepared baking tray, and bake until the crust is golden, about 35–40 minutes.

CHEESY TUNA AND CAULIFLOWER GRATIN

As written, the flavor profile of this dish is classic in its simplicity, but feel free to take the flavor to the next level by adding fresh herbs such as thyme or parsley to the cream sauce.

Serves 6

Avocado oil spray

1 large head cauliflower, cut into florets

6 ounces cream cheese, softened slightly

½ cup heavy whipping cream

¼ cup freshly grated Parmesan cheese

1 teaspoon salt

¼ teaspoon black pepper

1 small shallot, minced

2 (5-ounce) cans tuna in water, drained

1 cup shredded Cheddar cheese

½ cup Herbed Bread Crumbs (Chapter 2)

1 tablespoon minced fresh parsley, for garnish

Per Serving
Calories: 422 | Fat: 33 g
Protein: 21 g | Sodium: 894 mg
Fiber: 4 g | Carbohydrates: 13 g
Net Carbohydrates: 9 g | Sugar: 5 g

1 Preheat the oven to 400°F. Spray the inside of an 8" × 10" or similar size casserole dish with avocado oil.

2 Add the cauliflower to a large pot and cover by 3" with cold water. Bring to a boil, and then cook until the cauliflower is fork-tender, about 5–7 minutes. (Don't overcook because it'll soften more in the oven.) Drain well.

3 In a medium bowl, beat the cream cheese until smooth, and then beat in the cream, Parmesan, salt, black pepper, and shallot.

4 Once drained, add the cauliflower back to the pot it was cooked in and slightly mash it, leaving many large pieces. Stir in the cream sauce and then fold in the tuna.

5 Pour the cauliflower mixture into the prepared dish and spread it out. Sprinkle the Cheddar on top, and then sprinkle on the bread crumbs.

6 Bake until the cheese is melted and the casserole is hot, about 15–20 minutes.

7 Let the casserole sit 10 minutes, then sprinkle on the parsley and serve.

Lunches for the Week

This recipe is perfect for whipping up on the weekend and portioning out for lunches during the week! You can reheat it in a microwave or toaster oven (be sure to use an oven-safe container), or you can freeze it for up to three months and thaw to room temperature before reheating.

CHAPTER 6

SNACKS

SESAME ALMOND CRACKERS

If you like thin, buttery, almost flaky crackers, this recipe will be your new best friend. You can also add a teaspoon of fresh herbs, such as rosemary or thyme, to play with the flavor profile. They're wonderful as an all-purpose cracker and a great addition to a cheese or charcuterie board.

Serves 8

8 tablespoons unsalted butter, softened slightly
2 large egg whites
½ teaspoon salt
¼ teaspoon black pepper
2¼ cups almond flour
2 tablespoons sesame seeds

Per Serving
Calories: 299 | Fat: 28 g
Protein: 8 g | Sodium: 172 mg
Fiber: 4 g | Carbohydrates: 7 g
Net Carbohydrates: 4 g | Sugar: 1 g

1 Preheat the oven to 350°F.

2 In a large bowl, beat together the butter, egg whites, salt, and black pepper.

3 Stir in the almond flour and sesame seeds.

4 Roll the dough out between two pieces of parchment paper to a rectangle about the size of a half sheet pan (18" × 13").

5 Peel off the top piece of parchment paper and place the crackers (still on the bottom piece of parchment paper) onto a half sheet pan.

6 Use a ruler with a knife or pizza cutter to score the dough into crackers (to get forty-eight crackers, make six cuts lengthwise and eight cuts across).

7 Bake until golden, about 18–24 minutes, rotating the tray once halfway through.

8 Cool completely, and then break up the crackers where the dough was scored.

9 Store in an airtight container at room temperature up to two weeks.

SEEDY CRACKERS

These Seedy Crackers have three different kinds of seeds and tons of nutrients! We left the flavor profile basic, but you can add herbs, spices, or flavorings if you'd like. Taco seasoning, cinnamon and vanilla, or everything bagel seasoning are all flavor profiles that would work well here. Depending on how you flavor these crackers, serve them topped with your favorite cheese or jam.

Serves 4

1 teaspoon extra-virgin olive oil, plus more for your hands

½ cup golden flaxseed meal

½ cup raw sunflower seeds

1 tablespoon sesame seeds

1 large egg, lightly beaten

½ teaspoon salt

Per Serving

Calories: 199 | Fat: 16 g
Protein: 8 g | Sodium: 313 mg
Fiber: 6 g | Carbohydrates: 9 g
Net Carbohydrates: 3 g | Sugar: 1 g

1 Preheat the oven to 325°F. Line a large baking tray with a Silpat liner or parchment paper and drizzle on 1 teaspoon olive oil.

2 In a large bowl, stir together all ingredients until well combined.

3 Oil your hands, then press the dough out onto the prepared baking tray into an 8" circle.

4 Bake 15 minutes, and then carefully flip the slab over and bake an additional 15 minutes.

5 Let the cracker disk cool completely in the oven with the door ajar.

6 Once cooled, break into 1"–2" crackers (you'll get about sixteen crackers). The beauty of these crackers is that they should look rustic and all have a slightly different shape.

7 Serve crackers, or store in an airtight container at room temperature up to two weeks.

CHEDDAR CRACKERS

These Cheddar Crackers are a perfect addition to an appetizer platter, and are also perfect for munching on their own! They taste like a fancy version of Cheez-It crackers. We recommend using a good quality Cheddar because its flavor will really shine through.

Serves 8

4 tablespoons unsalted butter, softened slightly

1 large egg white

¼ teaspoon salt

1 cup plus 2 tablespoons almond flour

1 teaspoon minced fresh thyme

1 cup shredded sharp white Cheddar cheese

Per Serving
Calories: 200 | Fat: 18 g
Protein: 7 g | Sodium: 178 mg
Fiber: 2 g | Carbohydrates: 4 g
Net Carbohydrates: 2 g | Sugar: 1 g

1 Preheat the oven to 300°F.

2 In a large bowl, beat together the butter, egg white, and salt.

3 Stir in the almond flour and thyme and then the Cheddar until well incorporated.

4 Roll the dough out between two pieces of parchment paper to a rectangle about 11" long by 9" wide.

5 Peel off the top piece of parchment paper and place the crackers (still on the bottom piece of parchment paper) onto an 18" x 13" half sheet pan.

6 Use a ruler with a knife or pizza cutter to score the dough into crackers (you should get around thirty-two crackers).

7 Bake until golden, about 45–55 minutes, rotating the tray once halfway through.

8 Cool completely, and then break up the crackers where the dough was scored.

9 Store in an airtight container at room temperature up to two weeks.

Can I Use Dried Herbs Instead of Fresh?

Whenever possible try to use fresh herbs instead of dried because their flavor is much livelier, brighter, and, well, *fresher*! With that being said, sometimes dried is the only option and dried herbs are usually better than no herbs. The flavor of dried herbs is actually more concentrated than fresh, so you'll want to use about one third the amount of dried herbs as you would fresh.

SAVORY PARMESAN, GARLIC, AND HERB BISCOTTI

Who says biscotti has to be sweet and loaded with carbs to taste good?! Crisp and flavorful, these biscotti are delicious on their own for a crunchy snack, or use them any way you would eat a cracker.

Serves 5

⅔ cup almond flour

2 tablespoons golden flaxseed meal

2 tablespoons freshly grated Parmesan cheese

1 tablespoon coconut flour

1 teaspoon garlic powder

1 teaspoon dried Italian herb seasoning

¾ teaspoon baking powder

¼ teaspoon salt

⅛ teaspoon black pepper

2 tablespoons extra-virgin olive oil

2 large eggs

Per Serving
Calories: 194 | Fat: 17 g
Protein: 7 g | Sodium: 243 mg
Fiber: 3 g | Carbohydrates: 6 g
Net Carbohydrates: 3 g | Sugar: 1 g

1 Preheat the oven to 350°F. Line a large baking tray with parchment paper or a Silpat liner.

2 In a medium bowl, whisk together the almond flour, flaxseed meal, Parmesan, coconut flour, garlic powder, Italian herb seasoning, baking powder, salt, and black pepper.

3 Whisk in the olive oil, then whisk in the eggs. Let the batter sit 3 minutes to thicken slightly.

4 Pour the batter out onto the prepared baking tray and spread it out to a rectangle about 8"–9" long by 4"–5" wide. Bake for 10 minutes, and then remove from oven.

5 Turn the oven down to 300°F.

6 Cool the loaf for 10 minutes, then use a serrated knife to slice the loaf on a slight diagonal into ½"-thick slices (you should get about fifteen slices).

7 Arrange the biscotti on the baking tray and bake until golden, about 35 minutes, flipping the biscotti over once halfway through.

8 Turn off the oven and let the biscotti cool in the oven (leave the oven door closed, but check them and leave the oven door ajar if the biscotti start to get too dark).

9 Store the biscotti in an airtight container at room temperature up to one month.

GRAHAM CRACKERS

If you're looking for a slightly sweet, portable treat that doesn't need to be refrigerated, Graham Crackers are for you! Stash a bag of them in your purse for when you're out all day and need a quick bite, but don't have time to stop for food. Heads-up, kiddos love them too!

Serves 8

8 tablespoons unsalted butter, softened slightly
2 large egg whites
1½ teaspoons blackstrap molasses
1 teaspoon pure vanilla extract
14 drops liquid stevia
2¼ cups almond flour
4 tablespoons granulated erythritol
2 teaspoons ground cinnamon
½ teaspoon salt
⅛ teaspoon baking soda

Per Serving
Calories: 293 | Fat: 27 g
Protein: 8 g | Sodium: 192 mg
Fiber: 4 g | Carbohydrates: 14 g
Net Carbohydrates: 5 g | Sugar: 2 g

1 Preheat the oven to 325°F.

2 In a large bowl, beat together the butter, egg whites, blackstrap molasses, vanilla, and liquid stevia.

3 Stir in the almond flour, granulated erythritol, cinnamon, salt, and baking soda.

4 Roll the dough out between two pieces of parchment paper to a rectangle about the size of a half sheet pan (18" × 13").

5 Peel off the top piece of parchment paper and place the crackers (still on the bottom piece of parchment paper) onto a half sheet pan.

6 Use a ruler and a knife or pizza cutter to score the dough into crackers (to get forty-eight crackers, make six cuts lengthwise and eight cuts across).

7 Bake until golden, about 20 minutes, rotating the tray once halfway through.

8 Cool completely, then break up the crackers where the dough was scored.

9 Store in an airtight container at room temperature up to two weeks.

Blackstrap Molasses

Blackstrap molasses is a product of sugar refining, and it is surprisingly nutrient-dense! It contains vitamins and minerals such as vitamin B_6, iron, calcium, magnesium, manganese, potassium, and selenium. Blackstrap molasses is also higher in carbs, which is why we used it sparingly in this recipe to add depth of flavor and color, instead of as a sweetener.

BROCCOLI CHEDDAR HOT POCKETS

You've heard the expression "go big or go home," right? That was our motto when we came up with these Broccoli Cheddar Hot Pockets. Of course, you can cut the dough smaller and make twelve single-sized pastries if you prefer. These are addictive savory pastries filled with a cheesy broccoli filling—they'll have everyone in the family lining up to eat broccoli!

Yields 6 hot pockets | Serves 12

BROCCOLI CHEDDAR FILLING

1½ cups chopped broccoli
1 tablespoon unsalted butter
1 large clove garlic, minced
3 ounces cream cheese
¼ cup heavy whipping cream
½ teaspoon Dijon mustard
¼ teaspoon onion powder
¼ teaspoon hot sauce
⅛ teaspoon salt
⅛ teaspoon black pepper
1 cup shredded yellow Cheddar cheese

HOT POCKET CRUST

3 cups shredded low-moisture part-skim mozzarella cheese
2 ounces cream cheese
2 large eggs
1 teaspoon apple cider vinegar
3 drops liquid stevia
2 cups almond flour
2 teaspoons baking powder
Avocado oil, for your hands
1 large egg
1 tablespoon water

For the Broccoli Cheddar Filling:

1 Steam the broccoli for 2 minutes and drain well. Set aside.

2 In a small saucepan over low heat, heat the butter. Once melted, add the garlic and cook 30 seconds, stirring constantly. Add the cream cheese, cream, Dijon, onion powder, hot sauce, salt, and black pepper, whisking until smooth. Once smooth, whisk in the Cheddar a handful at a time (the Cheddar doesn't have to fully melt into the sauce). Turn off the heat and stir in the broccoli.

3 Cool to room temperature, and then refrigerate at least 2 hours.

For the Hot Pocket Crust:

1 In a large microwave-safe bowl, add the mozzarella and cream cheese. Microwave for 60 seconds, then give it a stir, and continue microwaving in 20-second increments until the cheese is fully melted and combined when stirred.

2 In a small bowl, whisk together the eggs, vinegar, and liquid stevia.

3 In a medium bowl, whisk together the almond flour and baking powder.

4 Stir the egg mixture into the melted cheese until combined, and then stir in the almond flour mixture until it forms a dough.

Per Serving

Calories: 317 | Fat: 26 g

Protein: 16 g | Sodium: 407 mg

Fiber: 2 g | Carbohydrates: 8 g

Net Carbohydrates: 5 g | Sugar: 2 g

5 Oil your hands and knead the dough until it comes together as a ball. Divide the dough into two equal portions, forming each into a ball.

6 Roll each ball of dough out between two pieces of parchment paper to a rectangle 12" long by 9" wide.

7 Cut each ball of dough once lengthwise down the middle, and three times crosswise, so you end up with a total of twelve rectangles of dough (six from each dough ball), each 6" long by 3" wide.

To Assemble and Bake:

1 Preheat the oven to 375°F. Line two large baking trays with Silpat liners or parchment paper.

2 Spoon 4 tablespoons chilled Broccoli Cheddar Filling onto each of six rectangles, spreading it in an even layer but leaving a ¼" border along the outside.

3 To seal each pastry, carefully pick up one rectangle of dough that doesn't have filling and place it directly on top of a pastry with filling. Lightly press down the edges to seal, and then use a fork to crimp. Continue this way until all six pastries are formed.

4 Carefully place the pastries on the prepared baking trays (use a metal spatula to help transfer them).

5 In a small bowl, whisk together the egg and water, and lightly brush the egg wash on top of each pastry (discard the extra egg wash). Cut four slits in the top of each pastry so steam can escape.

6 Bake until the pastries are golden, about 18–20 minutes, rotating the trays once halfway through. Serve warm.

CORN DOG BITES

Our Corn Dog Bites bring the best of ballpark food right to you, minus the carbs. These make a great appetizer or snack, and are always a hit with both kids and adults. Serve them with yellow mustard or sugar-free ketchup for dipping.

Serves 8

Avocado oil spray
1 cup almond flour
2 tablespoons coconut flour
1½ teaspoons baking powder
¼ teaspoon salt
¼ teaspoon garlic powder
¼ teaspoon onion powder
⅛ teaspoon black pepper
2 large eggs
¼ cup water
¼ cup heavy cream
6 tablespoons unsalted butter, melted and cooled slightly
4 organic uncured beef hot dogs

Per Serving
Calories: 243 | Fat: 23 g
Protein: 8 g | Sodium: 336 mg
Fiber: 2 g | Carbohydrates: 5 g
Net Carbohydrates: 3 g | Sugar: 1 g

1 Preheat the oven to 350°F. Lightly spray twenty-four wells of a mini muffin tray with avocado oil.

2 In a large bowl, whisk together the almond flour, coconut flour, baking powder, salt, garlic powder, onion powder, and black pepper.

3 In a medium bowl, whisk together the eggs, water, cream, and butter.

4 Stir the wet ingredients into the dry, and let the batter rest 3 minutes (it will thicken slightly).

5 Spoon the batter into the mini muffin wells.

6 Cut each hot dog into six equal pieces and place one in the center of each muffin well.

7 Bake until the Corn Dog Bites are golden along the outside, about 20 minutes.

8 Let the bites cool 10 minutes in the pan before removing.

What Are Uncured Hot Dogs?

Uncured hot dogs don't contain artificial preservatives to prevent spoiling and enhance the flavor. Instead, uncured hot dogs are preserved with some form of celery, which is a natural source of nitrates. You can find this information right on the package label.

PEPPERONI AND CHEESE CALZONES

These delicious calzones bring your favorite pizzeria right to your own kitchen! As they bake up, you'll think you walked into a pizza shop. If it fits into your macros, serve these up with a little cup of low-carb marinara for dipping.

Yields 4 calzones

Avocado oil, for your hands

1 batch Pizza Dough (Chapter 2)

4 tablespoons low-carb marinara sauce

6 tablespoons shredded mozzarella cheese

4 tablespoons diced pepperoni

1 large egg

1 tablespoon water

2 teaspoons dried Italian herb seasoning

Per Serving
Calories: 433 | Fat: 24 g
Protein: 24 g | Sodium: 668 mg
Fiber: 4 g | Carbohydrates: 12 g
Net Carbohydrates: 8 g | Sugar: 3 g

1 Preheat the oven to 425°F. Line a large baking sheet with parchment paper.

2 Oil your hands and knead the dough until it comes together as a ball. Divide the dough into four equal parts.

3 Roll each ball out between two pieces of parchment paper to make a circle, each 7" in diameter.

4 Add the following to half of each calzone: 1 tablespoon marinara, 1½ tablespoons mozzarella, and 1 tablespoon pepperoni.

5 Fold over the dough of each calzone and press to seal it closed. Transfer the calzones to the prepared baking sheet.

6 In a small bowl, beat the egg and water. Lightly brush the top of each calzone with the egg wash (discard the extra) and sprinkle the Italian herb seasoning on top.

7 Bake until golden, about 18–20 minutes. Serve warm.

PRETZEL BITES

These Pretzel Bites are addictively delicious with a fluffy bread-like texture, yeasty aroma, and melted butter and coarse salt on top. You can eat them as-is or serve them with your favorite cheese sauce for dipping. They are the perfect food for game day or any party!

Serves 8

1 teaspoon instant yeast
2 tablespoons warm water
1 cup almond flour
1 teaspoon psyllium husk powder
1 teaspoon baking powder
1½ cups shredded low-moisture part-skim mozzarella cheese
1 ounce cream cheese
1 large egg, lightly beaten
Avocado oil, for your hands
1 tablespoon unsalted butter, melted
½ teaspoon coarse kosher salt

Per Serving
Calories: 180 | Fat: 14 g
Protein: 9 g | Sodium: 332 mg
Fiber: 2 g | Carbohydrates: 5 g
Net Carbohydrates: 3 g | Sugar: 1 g

1 Preheat the oven to 425°F. Line a large baking sheet with parchment paper or a Silpat liner.

2 In a small bowl, add the yeast and warm water and stir to combine. Set aside until foamy, about 5–10 minutes.

3 In a medium bowl, whisk together the almond flour, psyllium husk powder, and baking powder. Set aside.

4 In a large microwave-safe bowl, add the mozzarella and cream cheese. Microwave for 60 seconds, then give it a stir, and continue microwaving in 20-second increments until the cheese is fully melted and combined when stirred.

5 Stir the foamy yeast mixture into the melted cheese until combined, and then stir in the beaten egg until combined. Stir in the almond flour mixture until it forms a dough.

6 Oil your hands and knead the dough until it comes together as a ball.

7 Divide the dough into four equal pieces. Roll each into a log about 4" long and cut each log into four bites, so you end up with sixteen bites total.

8 Arrange the bites on the prepared baking sheet and bake until golden, about 10 minutes.

9 As soon as they're out of the oven, brush the top of each Pretzel Bite with melted butter and sprinkle on a little kosher salt.

10 Cool slightly before serving.

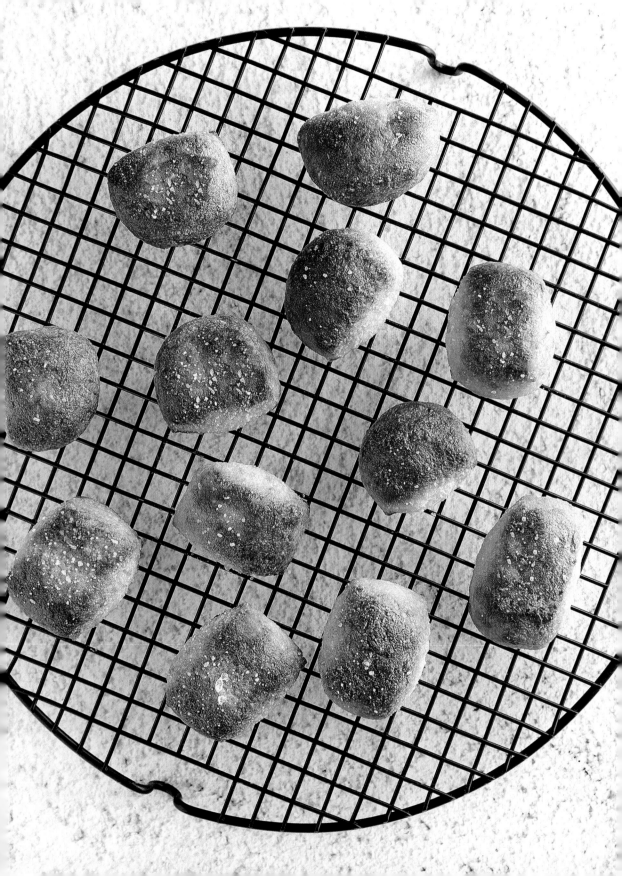

PIZZA MUFFIN BITES

These Pizza Muffin Bites pack all the flavor of pizza into perfect little bite-sized muffins. Make a batch of these on the weekend and keep them on hand for after-school snacks throughout the week.

Serves 6

Avocado oil spray
1 cup almond flour
2 tablespoons coconut flour
1½ teaspoons baking powder
½ teaspoon salt
¼ teaspoon black pepper
¼ teaspoon onion powder
2 large eggs
¼ cup water
¼ cup heavy whipping cream
4 tablespoons unsalted butter, melted and cooled slightly
1 teaspoon apple cider vinegar
5 drops liquid stevia
2 tablespoons no-sugar-added pizza sauce
¼ cup finely chopped pepperoni
6 tablespoons shredded mozzarella cheese
1½ teaspoons dried Italian herb seasoning

Per Serving
Calories: 295 | Fat: 27 g
Protein: 10 g | Sodium: 466 mg
Fiber: 3 g | Carbohydrates: 7 g
Net Carbohydrates: 4 g | Sugar: 1 g

1 Preheat the oven to 350°F. Lightly spray twenty-four wells of a mini muffin tray with avocado oil.

2 In a large bowl, whisk together the almond flour, coconut flour, baking powder, salt, black pepper, and onion powder.

3 In a medium bowl, whisk together the eggs, water, cream, butter, vinegar, and liquid stevia.

4 Stir the wet ingredients into the dry, and let the batter rest 3 minutes (it will thicken slightly).

5 Spoon the batter into the prepared mini muffin wells.

6 Top each muffin with ¼ teaspoon pizza sauce. Add the pepperoni on top of the sauce, and then top each with ¾ teaspoon mozzarella. Sprinkle the Italian herb seasoning on top.

7 Bake until the Pizza Muffin Bites are golden along the outside, about 15–20 minutes.

8 Let the bites cool 10 minutes in the muffin tray before removing.

GOAT CHEESE AND ZA'ATAR PINWHEELS

If you're looking for a classy appetizer for your next party or a fun new twist on rolls, you'll want to try these pinwheels. They're full of bright, zesty flavor, and were inspired by Middle Eastern savory pastries Faith used to eat while living in Jordan. Serve these with scrambled eggs for brunch, with a salad for lunch, or with grilled meat and steamed vegetables for dinner.

Serves 8

1 tablespoon unsalted butter

2 small onions, peeled and diced

1 teaspoon instant yeast

2 tablespoons warm water

1 cup almond flour

1 teaspoon psyllium husk powder

1 teaspoon baking powder

1½ cups shredded low-moisture part-skim mozzarella cheese

1 ounce cream cheese

1 large egg, lightly beaten

Avocado oil, olive oil, or ghee, for your hands

4 ounces crumbled goat cheese

2 tablespoons za'atar

1 Preheat the oven to 375°F. Line a large baking tray with parchment paper or a Silpat liner.

2 In a small skillet over medium to medium-low heat, heat the butter. Once melted, add the onion and cook until softened, about 5 minutes. Cool slightly.

3 In a small bowl, add the yeast and warm water and stir to combine. Set aside until foamy, about 5–10 minutes.

4 In a medium bowl, whisk together the almond flour, psyllium husk powder, and baking powder. Set aside.

5 In a large microwave-safe bowl, add the mozzarella and cream cheese. Microwave for 60 seconds, then give it a stir, and continue microwaving in 20-second increments until the cheese is fully melted and combined when stirred.

6 Stir the foamy yeast mixture into the melted cheese until combined, and then stir in the beaten egg until combined. Stir in the almond flour mixture until it forms a dough.

7 Oil your hands and knead the dough until it comes together as a ball.

8 Roll the dough out between two pieces of parchment paper to a rectangle about 12" long by 9" wide.

continued . . .

GOAT CHEESE AND ZA'ATAR PINWHEELS (CONTINUED)

Per Serving
Calories: 242 | Fat: 19 g
Protein: 13 g | Sodium: 241 mg
Fiber: 2 g | Carbohydrates: 7 g
Net Carbohydrates: 5 g | Sugar: 2 g

9 Spread the onion out on top of the dough, leaving a border of about ¼" along the outside. Sprinkle the goat cheese on top, and then sprinkle on the za'atar.

10 Use the parchment paper to help roll up the dough into a log. Freeze the log for 5 minutes, and then cut the log crosswise into eight equal pieces.

11 Spread the rolls out evenly on the prepared baking tray.

12 Bake until golden, about 24–26 minutes.

13 Cool slightly before serving.

What Is Za'atar?

Za'atar is a Middle Eastern spice blend that varies by region. Most mixes usually contain some combination of the following ingredients: thyme, oregano, marjoram, sumac, sesame seeds, and salt. You can find it easily at Middle Eastern grocery stores or specialty spice shops.

TORTILLA CHIPS

These chips are what your dips have been missing! We like to cook these Tortilla Chips until they're nice and golden and super-crispy. You can play with spice additions, such as garlic powder, onion powder, paprika, and so on, for different flavor profiles.

Serves 6

1½ cups shredded low-moisture part-skim mozzarella cheese
½ cup almond flour
1 tablespoon golden flaxseed meal
¼ teaspoon salt
⅛ teaspoon black pepper

Per Serving
Calories: 143 | Fat: 11 g
Protein: 9 g | Sodium: 289 mg
Fiber: 1 g | Carbohydrates: 4 g
Net Carbohydrates: 3 g | Sugar: 1 g

1 Preheat the oven to 375°F. Line two large baking sheets with parchment paper or Silpat liners.

2 In a large microwave-safe bowl, add the mozzarella. Microwave for 60 seconds, then give it a stir, and continue microwaving in 15-second increments until the cheese is fully melted and you can stir it together with a fork.

3 Once the cheese is melted, use a fork to mix in the almond flour, flaxseed meal, salt, and black pepper. Use your hands to knead it a bit until it looks like dough. (If the dough cools too much, you may need to microwave it for a few seconds so it's easier to work with.)

4 Divide the dough into two equal balls. Spread or roll each ball of dough out onto the prepared baking sheets until each is a rectangle about 8" × 10". Cut each into square- or triangle-shaped chips. Spread the chips out on the baking sheets so they're not touching.

5 Bake until golden brown on both sides, about 10–15 minutes, flipping the chips once halfway through.

6 Serve, or store the chips in an airtight container at room temperature up to three days. To recrisp the chips after the first day, bake them on a large baking sheet for 5 minutes at 350°F.

SPICED BEEF EMPANADAS

Next time you need a delicious keto appetizer, think about whipping up these Spiced Beef Empanadas! This recipe is great if you're feeding a crowd, and if not, they freeze and reheat well (thaw them to room temperature, and reheat them in a 400°F oven for about 5 minutes).

Serves 10

SPICED BEEF FILLING
1 pound 85% lean ground beef

1 medium onion, peeled and chopped

4 large cloves garlic, minced

½ cup water

1 tablespoon good-quality red wine vinegar

1 tablespoon tomato paste

1 teaspoon dried oregano

1 teaspoon dried thyme

1 teaspoon salt

½ teaspoon black pepper

½ teaspoon cumin

½ teaspoon sweet paprika

Pinch cayenne pepper

3 drops liquid stevia

3 tablespoons pimiento-stuffed green olives, halved

EMPANADA CRUST
4½ cups shredded low-moisture part-skim mozzarella cheese

3 ounces cream cheese

3 large eggs

1½ teaspoons apple cider vinegar

9 drops liquid stevia

3 cups almond flour

3 teaspoons baking powder

For the Spiced Beef Filling:

1 Heat a large skillet over medium-high heat. Once hot, add the beef and onion. Cook until browned, about 5–7 minutes, stirring occasionally to break up the meat.

2 Add the garlic and cook 30 seconds more, stirring constantly.

3 Stir in the water, red wine vinegar, tomato paste, oregano, thyme, salt, black pepper, cumin, sweet paprika, cayenne pepper, and liquid stevia.

4 Cover the skillet, turn the heat down to simmer, and cook 20 minutes, stirring occasionally. If the sauce needs additional thickening, cook it uncovered for a few minutes, stirring frequently, until it reaches your desired consistency.

5 Turn off the heat and stir in the olives.

For the Empanada Crust:

1 In a large microwave-safe bowl, add the mozzarella and cream cheese. Microwave for 60 seconds, then give it a stir, and continue microwaving in 20-second increments until the cheese is fully melted and combined when stirred.

2 In a small bowl, whisk together the eggs, apple cider vinegar, and liquid stevia.

3 In a medium bowl, whisk together the almond flour and baking powder.

4 Stir the egg mixture into the melted cheese until combined, and then stir in the almond flour mixture until it forms a dough.

continued . . .

SPICED BEEF EMPANADAS (CONTINUED)

OTHER

Avocado oil, for your hands

1 large egg

1 tablespoon water

Per Serving

Calories: 491 | Fat: 37 g
Protein: 31 g | Sodium: 815 mg
Fiber: 4 g | Carbohydrates: 13 g
Net Carbohydrates: 9 g | Sugar: 3 g

5 Oil your hands and knead the dough until it comes together as a ball. Divide the dough into three equal portions.

6 Roll each ball of dough out between two pieces of parchment paper to a circle about 11" in diameter.

7 Use a 3" biscuit cutter to stamp out the dough into circles, gathering and re-rolling the dough as necessary (you should get thirty-eight to forty dough circles).

To Assemble and Bake:

1 Preheat the oven to 375°F. Line two large baking trays with Silpat liners or parchment paper.

2 Place 2 teaspoons Spiced Beef Filling in the center of each dough circle and gently fold the dough over onto itself to close up the filling, pressing the seam together. Arrange the empanadas on the prepared baking sheets about ½" apart and use a fork to crimp the seam.

3 In a small bowl, whisk together the egg and water, and lightly brush the egg wash on top of each pastry (discard the extra egg wash). Cut two slits in the top of each empanada so steam can escape.

4 Bake until the empanadas are golden, about 15–18 minutes, rotating the trays once halfway through.

5 Serve warm.

MUSHROOM AND THYME GALETTES

For an elegant appetizer party featuring all keto foods, get a couple wedges of your favorite cheeses, an assortment of olives, a couple different kinds of nuts, roasted bell peppers, and fresh herbs to tuck in between everything for color and aroma. Then whip up these Mushroom and Thyme Galettes and your guests are sure to be impressed!

Serves 6

MUSHROOM AND THYME FILLING

1½ tablespoons unsalted butter

6 ounces button mushrooms, sliced

1 large clove garlic, minced

1 teaspoon minced fresh thyme

Pinch salt

Pinch black pepper

½ cup shredded sharp white Cheddar cheese

GALETTE CRUST

½ teaspoon beef gelatin

1 tablespoon boiling water

½ teaspoon apple cider vinegar

3 drops liquid stevia

1 large egg white

1½ cups almond flour

¼ teaspoon plus ⅛ teaspoon salt

2 tablespoons chilled unsalted butter, diced

1 large egg

1 tablespoon water

For the Mushroom and Thyme Filling:

1 Preheat a large skillet over medium heat. Add the butter and once melted, add the mushrooms and cook until softened, about 8–10 minutes, stirring occasionally.

2 Add the garlic, thyme, salt, and black pepper and cook 1 minute more, stirring constantly. Turn off the heat and cool to room temperature.

3 Stir the Cheddar into the mushroom mixture and refrigerate to chill, about 15 minutes.

For the Galette Crust:

1 In a small bowl, add the beef gelatin and boiling water, stir to dissolve, and cool a few minutes until lukewarm. Whisk in the vinegar, liquid stevia, and egg white.

2 In a large bowl, whisk together the almond flour and salt.

3 Use a fork to mix the egg white mixture into the dry ingredients, and then cut in the butter until it forms a crumbly dough.

4 Gently press the dough together to form a disk. Wrap in plastic wrap and refrigerate until well chilled, at least 2 hours (or up to three days).

To Assemble and Bake:

1 Preheat the oven to 350°F. Line a large baking tray with a Silpat liner or parchment paper.

continued . . .

MUSHROOM AND THYME GALETTES (CONTINUED)

Per Serving
Calories: 280 | Fat: 25 g
Protein: 11 g | Sodium: 289 mg
Fiber: 3 g | Carbohydrates: 8 g
Net Carbohydrates: 5 g | Sugar: 2 g

2 Divide the dough into six equal pieces. Roll each into a ball, and then roll the balls out between two sheets of parchment paper into a circle about 4"–5" in diameter.

3 Use a thin metal spatula or pastry scraper to transfer the dough circles to the prepared baking tray, arranging them so they don't touch.

4 Divide the mushroom filling between the six dough circles, putting the filling in the center of each.

5 Gently use a thin metal spatula to fold the outer part of the dough circle up partway over the filling, molding the dough so it's smooth. (These pastries should not be completely covered in dough; they are open on top.) If the dough cracks a bit, you can gently mold and pinch it together. If the dough is very hard to work with, pop everything into the freezer to chill for 5 minutes.

6 Once all the galettes are formed, transfer the baking tray to the freezer to chill for 5 minutes.

7 In a small bowl, whisk together the egg and water, and lightly brush the egg wash on each crust (discard the extra egg wash).

8 Bake until the galettes are golden, about 20 minutes.

9 Serve hot, warm, or at room temperature.

What Is a Galette?

What we tend to think of as a galette is typically a free-form rustic pastry that can have either a sweet or savory filling. The outer rim of the pastry is folded over the filling to create a crust along the outside, but the top portion of the filling is open. Because each galette is hand shaped, each is slightly unique.

SWEET CHOCOLATE HAZELNUT BISCOTTI

We mastered the art of perfectly crisp biscotti with these Sweet Chocolate Hazelnut Biscotti! Not many keto foods have crunch, so if that's what you're craving you're in for a wonderful surprise. Soften them up by dunking them in your coffee or eat them as is for a breakfast with a crunch factor!

Serves 12

⅔ cup almond flour

5 tablespoons granulated monk fruit/erythritol blend

2 tablespoons golden flaxseed meal

1 tablespoon coconut flour

¾ teaspoon baking powder

¼ teaspoon salt

3 tablespoons unsalted butter, melted

15 drops liquid stevia

2 large eggs

¾ teaspoon pure vanilla extract

¼ teaspoon pure almond extract

½ cup chopped hazelnuts

⅓ cup stevia-sweetened chocolate chips

1 Preheat the oven to 300°F. Line a large baking tray with parchment paper or a Silpat liner.

2 In a medium bowl, whisk together the almond flour, granulated monk fruit/erythritol blend, flaxseed meal, coconut flour, baking powder, and salt.

3 In a separate medium bowl, combine the melted butter, liquid stevia, eggs, vanilla, and almond extract.

4 Stir the butter mixture into the almond flour mixture.

5 Place a piece of plastic wrap directly on top of the dough and chill in the freezer for 8 minutes.

6 Stir in the chopped hazelnuts and chocolate chips.

7 Pour the batter out onto the prepared baking tray and spread it out to a rectangle about 8"–9" long by 4"–5" wide. Bake 30 minutes.

8 Remove from oven and cool for 15 minutes.

9 Cut into ½"-thick slices, and place them back on the baking tray.

10 Bake another 30 minutes, flipping the biscotti over once halfway through.

continued...

SWEET CHOCOLATE HAZELNUT BISCOTTI (CONTINUED)

Per Serving
Calories: 135 | Fat: 12 g
Protein: 4 g | Sodium: 87 mg
Fiber: 3 g | Carbohydrates: 12 g
Net Carbohydrates: 4 g | Sugar: 1 g

11 Turn off the oven and leave the biscotti inside with the oven door closed until they're golden, about 5 minutes.

12 Let the biscotti cool to room temperature before serving (they will crisp upon cooling).

Can I Use a Chocolate Bar Instead of Chocolate Chips Here?

Unfortunately, for this recipe a chopped chocolate bar won't work as a good substitute for chocolate chips. This is because the chopped chocolate will melt too much and when you go to slice the biscotti you won't get pretty cuts; you'll get streaks of melted chocolate and a gooey mess.

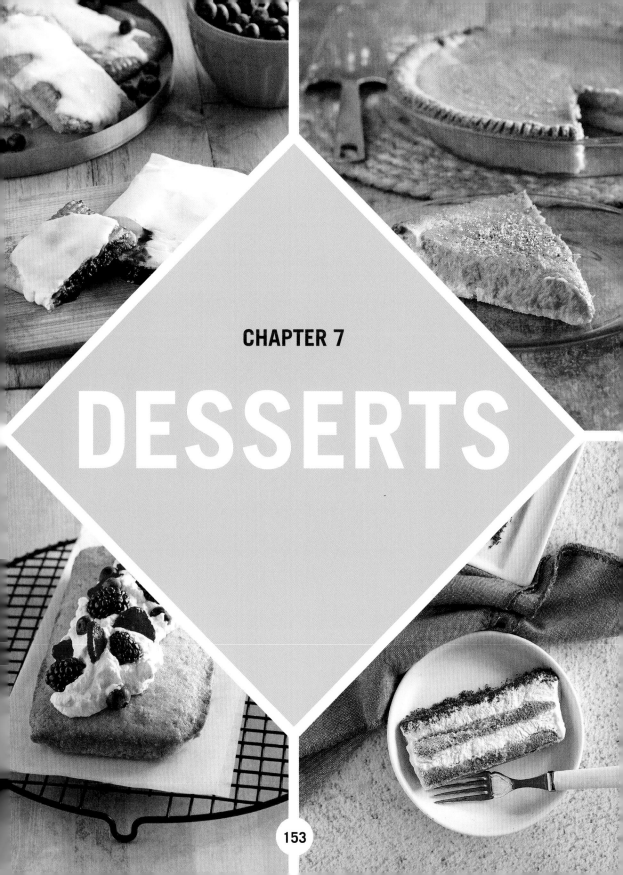

CHAPTER 7

DESSERTS

CLASSIC YELLOW BUTTER CAKE

We fully support the idea that some occasions require cake. This Classic Yellow Butter Cake is moist and tender-crumbed, and aromatic with vanilla and butter. It's sure to become your go-to when you want cake.

Yields 1 (9" x 5") cake | Serves 8

Coconut oil spray

6 tablespoons unsalted butter, at room temperature

4 tablespoons granulated erythritol

2 large eggs

1½ teaspoons pure vanilla extract

½ teaspoon pure almond extract

¼ teaspoon stevia glycerite

1 cup almond flour

2 tablespoons golden flaxseed meal

2 tablespoons tapioca flour

1 teaspoon baking powder

¼ teaspoon salt

½ cup heavy whipping cream, whipped to soft peaks

½ cup fresh blueberries, strawberries, or raspberries, for garnish

Per Serving
Calories: 249 | Fat: 23 g
Protein: 5 g | Sodium: 147 mg
Fiber: 2 g | Carbohydrates: 13 g
Net Carbohydrates: 5 g | Sugar: 2 g

1 Preheat the oven to 350°F. Line a 9" × 5" loaf pan with two pieces of parchment paper so it hangs over all four sides (so you can lift the cake out later). Lightly spray the inside with coconut oil.

2 In a large bowl, cream together the butter and granulated erythritol, and then beat in the eggs, vanilla, almond extract, and stevia glycerite.

3 In a medium bowl, whisk together the almond flour, flaxseed meal, tapioca flour, baking powder, and salt.

4 Beat the dry ingredients into the wet ingredients all at once.

5 Pour the batter into the prepared pan and spread it out. Bake until the cake is puffed and golden brown along the outside, about 27–32 minutes.

6 Cool and then top with whipped cream and berries. Cut into eight pieces.

7 Store leftovers covered in the refrigerator up to one week.

BERRIES AND CREAM CREPE CAKE

Whether you make this beautiful crepe cake for a special brunch or fancy dessert, it's sure to put a smile on everyone's face. Slightly sweet, buttery, vanilla-scented Crepes are layered with whipped cream and berries for a treat everyone will love.

Serves 8

1 cup heavy whipping cream
¼ teaspoon pure vanilla extract
5 drops liquid stevia
1 batch Crepes (Chapter 2)
½ cup fresh blackberries
½ cup fresh red raspberries

Per Serving
Calories: 391 | Fat: 37 g
Protein: 8 g | Sodium: 364 mg
Fiber: 5 g | Carbohydrates: 9 g
Net Carbohydrates: 5 g | Sugar: 3 g

1 In a medium bowl, whip the cream, vanilla, and liquid stevia until it forms soft peaks.

2 Place a Crepe in the center of a platter and spread a thin layer of whipped cream on top. Top with another Crepe and more whipped cream, and continue until the Crepes and whipped cream are gone.

3 Add the berries on top and serve immediately.

If You're Lactose Intolerant...

Use coconut oil instead of butter to make the Crepes. Instead of heavy whipping cream, use coconut whipped cream to layer the Crepes. This version is also Paleo!

CREAM CHEESE STRAWBERRY DANISH

These Cream Cheese Strawberry Danish only taste like an indulgence! They're great to meal prep over the weekend so you have breakfast ready for busy mornings, or a last-minute dessert on hand to indulge your sweet tooth. You can switch out the jam flavor and never get bored with them!

Yields 18 Danish

Coconut oil spray

6 large eggs

½ teaspoon cream of tartar

6 ounces cream cheese, softened slightly

2 tablespoons heavy cream

2 teaspoons pure vanilla extract

1 teaspoon apple cider vinegar

½ teaspoon liquid stevia

½ cup unflavored whey protein powder

½ tablespoon psyllium husk powder

¼ teaspoon salt

¼ teaspoon baking soda

6 ounces cream cheese, cut into eighteen pieces

3 tablespoons low-carb strawberry jam

Per Serving
Calories: 125 | Fat: 9 g
Protein: 8 g | Sodium: 130 mg
Fiber: 0 g | Carbohydrates: 4 g
Net Carbohydrates: 2 g | Sugar: 1 g

1 Preheat the oven to 375°F. Spray eighteen wells of a muffin tray with coconut oil.

2 Separate the egg whites from the yolks, placing the whites and yolks in two separate large bowls.

3 Add the cream of tartar to the bowl with the egg whites. Use a handheld electric mixer to beat until the egg whites form stiff peaks. Set aside.

4 To the bowl with the egg yolks, add the cream cheese, cream, vanilla, vinegar, and liquid stevia. Beat until well combined. Add the whey protein powder, psyllium husk powder, salt, and baking soda and beat until smooth.

5 Fold the egg whites into the egg yolk mixture a little at a time, being careful not to deflate the whites (a few streaks or lumps of egg whites are fine).

6 Divide the batter between the muffin wells.

7 Bake for 10 minutes. Carefully remove the muffin tray. Add a piece of cream cheese and ½ teaspoon jam on top of each pastry, lightly pressing it down.

8 Return to the oven and bake until golden, about 10 minutes more.

9 Cool in the pan for 5 minutes, and then run a paring knife along the outside of each pastry to remove them.

TIRAMISU

If you thought making homemade Tiramisu was too hard, this recipe will show you otherwise! For the best flavor, let this Tiramisu refrigerate twenty-four hours before serving. This sweet treat is decadent and rich, and perfect for when you need a special occasion dessert!

Yields 1 (9" × 5") loaf | Serves 12

LADYFINGERS
1 Classic Yellow Butter Cake
(see recipe in this chapter)

MASCARPONE MIXTURE
3 large eggs
4 tablespoons powdered erythritol
8 ounces mascarpone cheese
¼ cup heavy whipping cream
1 tablespoon dark rum
2 teaspoons pure vanilla extract
¼ teaspoon almond extract
⅛ teaspoon stevia glycerite
Pinch salt

OTHER
¾ cup strong espresso, cooled
10 drops liquid stevia
½ ounce 90% dark chocolate, finely grated

For the Ladyfingers:

1 Slice the Classic Yellow Butter Cake crosswise into ten equal slices, each about ½" thick.

2 Arrange the cake slices in an even layer on a large baking sheet and bake at 300°F until golden, about 50 minutes, flipping once halfway through.

3 Cool the cake slices.

For the Mascarpone Mixture:

1 Separate the egg yolks from the egg whites, placing the yolks and whites in two separate large bowls.

2 Beat the egg whites until they form stiff peaks, and set aside.

3 Beat the egg yolks with the powdered erythritol, mascarpone, cream, rum, vanilla, almond extract, stevia glycerite, and salt until thick and creamy.

4 Fold the egg white mixture into the egg yolk mixture, being careful not to overmix.

To Assemble:

1 Line a 9" × 5" loaf pan with parchment paper so you can easily pull out the Tiramisu later.

2 In a medium shallow bowl, combine the espresso and liquid stevia.

3 Dip five Ladyfingers in the espresso mixture, and arrange them in an even layer in the bottom of the prepared loaf pan. You may need to cut them so they don't overlap.

continued . . .

TIRAMISU (CONTINUED)

Per Serving
Calories: 293 | Fat: 28 g
Protein: 7 g | Sodium: 141 mg
Fiber: 2 g | Carbohydrates: 14 g
Net Carbohydrates: 4 g | Sugar: 2 g

4 Spread half of the Mascarpone Mixture on top.

5 Top with five more Ladyfingers dipped in espresso.

6 Spread the remaining Mascarpone Mixture on top.

7 Sprinkle on the grated chocolate.

8 Transfer to the refrigerator to set for 8 hours or overnight.

To Serve:

Use the parchment paper to lift out the Tiramisu and cut it crosswise into slices.

CREAM CHEESE MOUSSE TART

Ethereally light and fluffy, this tart makes a fantastic dessert any time of year. In the summertime, serve it with your favorite low-carb jam spooned on top. For a fun and festive twist around the holidays, add 1 teaspoon pure peppermint extract and ½ cup chopped 90% dark chocolate!

Serves 12

12 ounces cream cheese, softened slightly

4 tablespoons powdered erythritol

2 teaspoons pure vanilla extract

½ teaspoon vanilla bean paste

¼ teaspoon stevia glycerite

¼ teaspoon beef gelatin

2 teaspoons boiling water

1 cup heavy whipping cream, whipped to stiff peaks

1 Press-In Sweet Crust (Chapter 2), pre-baked in a 7" springform pan and cooled

Per Serving
Calories: 296 | Fat: 29 g
Protein: 6 g | Sodium: 149 mg
Fiber: 2 g | Carbohydrates: 10 g
Net Carbohydrates: 4 g | Sugar: 2 g

1 In a large bowl, beat together the cream cheese, powdered erythritol, vanilla extract, vanilla bean paste, and stevia glycerite.

2 In a small bowl, combine the beef gelatin and boiling water and stir to dissolve.

3 Beat the dissolved gelatin into the cream cheese mixture.

4 Beat one quarter of the whipped cream into the cream cheese mixture. Fold the remaining whipped cream into the cream cheese mixture one quarter at a time, being careful not to overmix.

5 Pour the cream cheese mousse into the pre-baked and cooled Press-In Sweet Crust. Cover and refrigerate until the tart is set, about 4 hours.

6 Store leftovers wrapped in the refrigerator up to five days.

Can You Omit the Beef Gelatin?

The beef gelatin helps this tart set a little firmer—not nearly as firm as Jell-O, but just a touch more stable. You can omit the gelatin (and the boiling water to dissolve it), but the end result will be a bit softer.

FRENCH SILK PIE

Every component of this pie is bakery quality: the buttery crust, the rich Chocolate Custard, and the vanilla-scented, slightly sweetened whipped cream. The end result is a truly show-stopping dessert! We use a little beef gelatin in the Whipped Cream Topping to help make it a little more stable and a little less likely to deflate.

Yields 1 (9") pie | Serves 12

CHOCOLATE CUSTARD

1½ cups heavy whipping cream
¾ cup powdered erythritol
¼ teaspoon stevia glycerite
⅛ teaspoon salt
3 large egg yolks
½ teaspoon beef gelatin
1 tablespoon boiling water
1½ teaspoons pure vanilla extract
3½ ounces 90% dark chocolate, chopped
1 Press-In Sweet Crust (Chapter 2), pre-baked in a 9" pie plate and cooled

WHIPPED CREAM TOPPING

1 cup heavy whipping cream
½ teaspoon beef gelatin
1 tablespoon boiling water
1 tablespoon powdered erythritol
½ teaspoon pure vanilla extract
7 drops liquid stevia
1 tablespoon 90% dark chocolate curls, for garnish

For the Chocolate Custard:

1   In a medium saucepan over medium heat, heat the cream, powdered erythritol, stevia glycerite, and salt until it's steaming and starting to bubble around the outside.

2   In a medium bowl, whisk 1 cup of the steaming hot cream mixture into the egg yolks, starting with just a couple drops at first and gradually whisking in the whole 1 cup.

3   Pour the tempered egg yolk mixture into the cream mixture. Turn the heat down to low and cook until it boils, stirring constantly. Immediately turn off the heat.

4   In a small bowl, add the beef gelatin and boiling water and stir to dissolve.

5   Whisk the dissolved beef gelatin, vanilla, and chopped chocolate into the custard until smooth.

6   Strain the custard through a fine-mesh sieve.

7   Pour the custard into the pre-baked and cooled pie crust. Cover and refrigerate until the custard is set, about 4 hours.

For the Whipped Cream Topping:

1   In a large bowl, beat the cream until it forms stiff peaks.

2   In a small bowl, add the beef gelatin and boiling water and stir to dissolve. Cool to room temperature.

3   Add the dissolved room temperature gelatin mixture, powdered erythritol, vanilla, and liquid stevia to the whipped cream and beat to combine.

Per Serving

Calories: 346 | Fat: 34 g

Protein: 6 g | Sodium: 95 mg

Fiber: 4 g | Carbohydrates: 25 g

Net Carbohydrates: 7 g | Sugar: 2 g

To Assemble:

1 Spoon or pipe the Whipped Cream Topping onto the set custard and sprinkle the chocolate curls on top.

2 Serve immediately, or refrigerate 2 hours so the whipped topping can set.

BLUEBERRY BREAKFAST PASTRIES

The beautiful thing about breakfast pastries is that you can fill them with any flavor of jam you like. Blueberry is a classic, but strawberry comes in at a close second. We actually prefer these without the icing, but if you're an icing person, you'll love these as-is! This recipe makes six very large pastries, so each serving is half a pastry.

Yields 6 large pastries | Serves 12

BLUEBERRY FILLING

1½ cups frozen blueberries

4 tablespoons powdered erythritol

½ tablespoon good-quality red wine vinegar

⅛ teaspoon stevia glycerite

⅛ teaspoon salt

1¼ teaspoons powdered fruit pectin

CRUST

3 cups shredded low-moisture part-skim mozzarella cheese

2 ounces cream cheese

3 large eggs, divided

1 teaspoon apple cider vinegar

10 drops liquid stevia

½ teaspoon pure vanilla extract

2 cups almond flour

2 teaspoons baking powder

Coconut oil spray, for your hands

1 tablespoon water

VANILLA ICING

¾ cup powdered erythritol

3 tablespoons heavy whipping cream

1 tablespoon fresh lemon juice

2 teaspoons water

¼ teaspoon pure vanilla extract

Pinch salt

For the Blueberry Filling:

In a medium saucepan over medium heat, add the frozen blueberries, powdered erythritol, red wine vinegar, stevia glycerite, and salt. Cover the saucepan and cook 10 minutes. Turn off the heat and stir in the pectin. Cool to room temperature, and then refrigerate to chill, about 30 minutes.

For the Crust:

1 In a large microwave-safe bowl, add the mozzarella and cream cheese. Microwave for 60 seconds, then give it a stir, and continue microwaving in 20-second increments until the cheese is fully melted and combined when stirred.

2 In a small bowl, whisk together two eggs, the apple cider vinegar, liquid stevia, and vanilla.

3 In a medium bowl, whisk together the almond flour and baking powder.

4 Stir the egg mixture into the melted cheese until combined, and then stir in the almond flour mixture until it forms a dough.

5 Oil your hands and knead the dough until it comes together as a ball. Divide the dough into two equal portions, forming each into a ball.

6 Roll each ball of dough out between two pieces of parchment paper to a rectangle 12" long by 9" wide.

7 Cut each rectangle in half widthwise, creating two (9" × 6") sections. Then cut each section widthwise into thirds, creating a total of six (6" × 3") rectangles.

continued . . .

BLUEBERRY BREAKFAST PASTRIES (CONTINUED)

Per Serving

Calories: 250 | Fat: 19 g
Protein: 13 g | Sodium: 326 mg
Fiber: 3 g | Carbohydrates: 25 g
Net Carbohydrates: 6 g | Sugar: 3 g

To Assemble and Bake:

1 Preheat the oven to 375°F. Line two large baking trays with Silpat liners or parchment paper.

2 Spoon 2 tablespoons chilled blueberry jam onto each of the six rectangles, spreading it in an even layer but leaving a ¼" border along the outside.

3 To seal each pastry, carefully pick up one rectangle of dough that doesn't have filling and place it directly on top of a pastry with filling. Lightly press down the edges to seal, and then use a fork to crimp. Continue this way until all six pastries are formed.

4 Carefully place the pastries on the prepared baking trays (use a metal spatula to help transfer them).

5 In a small bowl, whisk together the remaining egg and water, and lightly brush the egg wash on top of each pastry (discard the extra egg wash). Cut four slits in the top of each pastry so steam can escape.

6 Bake until the pastries are golden, about 18–20 minutes, rotating the trays once halfway through. Cool the pastries completely before icing.

For the Vanilla Icing:

1 In a small bowl, stir together all ingredients for the icing.

2 Spread the icing onto the cooled pastries and let it harden before serving.

CLASSIC CHEESECAKE

If you don't tell people this recipe is keto, they'd never guess. Serve it with your favorite low-carb strawberry sauce for topping.

Yields 1 (7") cheesecake | Serves 10

1 Press-In Sweet Crust (Chapter 2)

16 ounces cream cheese, softened slightly

½ cup heavy whipping cream

2 large eggs

5 tablespoons powdered erythritol

1 tablespoon pure vanilla extract

1 teaspoon fresh lemon juice

¼ teaspoon stevia glycerite

Per Serving
Calories: 369 | Fat: 35 g
Protein: 8 g | Sodium: 225 mg
Fiber: 2 g | Carbohydrates: 14 g
Net Carbohydrates: 5 g | Sugar: 3 g

1 Preheat the oven to 325°F.

2 Wrap the outside of a 7" springform pan with two pieces of aluminum foil before pressing the crust inside. Pre-bake the crust for 8 minutes.

3 Meanwhile, make the filling. In a large bowl, beat the cream cheese until smooth, and then beat in the cream, eggs, powdered erythritol, vanilla, lemon juice, and stevia glycerite until the mixture is smooth and creamy.

4 Place the pre-baked crust (still in the springform pan) into the bottom of a 9" × 13" casserole dish. Pour the cheesecake filling into the crust. Transfer this to the middle rack of the oven.

5 Carefully pour boiling water about one third to one half of the way up the outside of the springform pan.

6 Bake until the outside of the cheesecake is set but the center still jiggles, about 50 minutes.

7 Remove the cheesecake from the oven and let it cool in the water bath 30 minutes.

8 Cool to room temperature, and then refrigerate to chill (about 4 hours or overnight) before slicing.

Why Is My Cream Cheese Lumpy?

It can be hard to beat the lumps out of cream cheese, but we have a few tips. Start with room-temperature cream cheese. Beat the cream cheese by itself, so you can beat it for as long as it takes. Use a handheld electric mixer or stand mixer with the whisk attachment to beat it. If nothing else is working, it helps to warm the cream cheese slightly in a double boiler or microwave.

COCONUT CREAM PIE WITH GRAHAM CRACKER CRUST

This favorite diner dessert is now sure to be a staple in your keto pie rotation. For this pie, we crush our Graham Crackers (Chapter 6) to make crumbs for the crust. But if you're pressed for time, you can skip the crust and serve the Coconut Custard in individual cups topped with a dollop of whipped cream.

Yields 1 (9") pie | Serves 12

GRAHAM CRACKER CRUST
2 cups Graham Cracker crumbs (Chapter 6)

2 tablespoons granulated erythritol

Pinch salt

6 tablespoons unsalted butter, melted

7 drops liquid stevia

COCONUT CUSTARD
1¼ cups heavy whipping cream

½ cup water

3 tablespoons granulated erythritol

⅛ teaspoon stevia glycerite

⅛ teaspoon salt

8 large egg yolks

¾ teaspoon beef gelatin

2 tablespoons boiling water

1½ teaspoons pure vanilla extract

1½ teaspoons coconut extract

½ cup unsweetened shredded coconut

For the Graham Cracker Crust:

1 Preheat the oven to 350°F.

2 In a large bowl, use a fork to combine the Graham Cracker crumbs, granulated erythritol, and salt.

3 Add the melted butter and liquid stevia and stir until crumbly.

4 Press the Graham Cracker mixture into the bottom and up the sides of a 9" pie plate.

5 Bake 12 minutes, and then cool to room temperature.

For the Coconut Custard:

1 In a medium saucepan over medium heat, heat the cream, water, granulated erythritol, stevia glycerite, and salt until it's steaming and starting to bubble around the outside.

2 In a medium bowl, whisk 1 cup of the steaming hot cream mixture into the egg yolks, starting with just a couple drops at first and gradually whisking in the whole 1 cup.

3 Pour the tempered egg yolk mixture into the cream mixture. Turn the heat down to low and cook until it boils, stirring constantly. Immediately turn off the heat.

4 In a small bowl, add the beef gelatin and boiling water and stir to dissolve.

WHIPPED CREAM TOPPING
1 cup heavy whipping cream
½ teaspoon beef gelatin
1 tablespoon boiling water
1 tablespoon powdered erythritol
½ teaspoon pure vanilla extract
7 drops liquid stevia

GARNISH
1 tablespoon unsweetened shredded coconut, toasted and cooled

Per Serving
Calories: 366 | Fat: 37 g
Protein: 6 g | Sodium: 121 mg
Fiber: 2 g | Carbohydrates: 13 g
Net Carbohydrates: 4 g | Sugar: 2 g

5 Whisk the dissolved beef gelatin, vanilla, and coconut extract into the custard until smooth.

6 Strain the custard through a fine-mesh sieve.

7 Stir in the shredded coconut.

8 Pour the custard into the pre-baked and cooled pie crust. Cover and refrigerate until the custard is set, about 4 hours.

For the Whipped Cream Topping:

1 In a large bowl, beat the cream until it forms stiff peaks.

2 In a small bowl, add the beef gelatin and boiling water and stir to dissolve. Cool to room temperature.

3 Add the room temperature gelatin mixture, powdered erythritol, vanilla, and liquid stevia to the whipped cream and beat to combine.

To Assemble:

1 Spoon or pipe the Whipped Cream Topping onto the set custard and sprinkle the toasted coconut on top.

2 Serve immediately, or refrigerate 2 hours so the whipped topping can set.

Desiccated Coconut or Shredded Coconut?

Desiccated coconut and shredded coconut have a slightly different moisture level and size. Desiccated coconut is a bit drier and more finely ground. You can use either desiccated coconut or coconut flakes for this recipe, but make sure whatever you use is unsweetened to avoid added sugar.

PUMPKIN PIE

For so many of us, the holidays just wouldn't be the same without our favorite pie! We wanted to show that keto pie can be every bit as delicious as regular pie. Put it to the test and try this pie out for yourself!

Yields 1 (9") pie | Serves 12

1 batch All-Purpose Roll-Out Crust for Pies (Chapter 2), chilled

1 (15-ounce) can unsweetened pumpkin purée

2 large whole eggs

2 large egg yolks

¾ cup heavy whipping cream

½ cup powdered erythritol

2 teaspoons pumpkin pie spice

2 teaspoons pure vanilla extract

1 teaspoon blackstrap molasses

¼ teaspoon stevia glycerite

¼ teaspoon salt

Per Serving
Calories: 169 | Fat: 14 g
Protein: 5 g | Sodium: 173 mg
Fiber: 2 g | Carbohydrates: 14 g
Net Carbohydrates: 4 g | Sugar: 3 g

1 Preheat the oven to 350°F.

2 While it's still chilled, roll out the dough between two sheets of parchment paper to a circle about 10" in diameter.

3 Remove the top sheet of parchment paper from the dough, and pick up the bottom sheet of parchment that the rolled-out dough is on. Gently flip the dough over, inverting it into a 9" pie plate. Press the crust into the bottom and up the sides of the pie plate, crimping the dough at the top. Use a fork to poke holes in the bottom of the crust.

4 Bake the crust (with nothing in it) for 5 minutes.

5 In a large bowl, beat together the pumpkin, eggs, egg yolks, cream, powdered erythritol, pumpkin pie spice, vanilla, molasses, stevia glycerite, and salt until well combined.

6 Pour the pumpkin mixture into the crust.

7 Bake until the filling is set along the outside, but still jiggly in the center, about 40 minutes. If the crust starts to get too dark before the filling is cooked, you can cover the crust with aluminum foil to prevent burning.

8 Cool before slicing.

What's in Pumpkin Pie Spice?

Pumpkin pie spice is a spice blend that usually contains the following: cinnamon, nutmeg, ginger, allspice, and cloves. It's available at regular grocery stores, but you can easily make your own and customize it by varying the amount of each spice to suit your taste preferences!

US/METRIC CONVERSION CHART

VOLUME CONVERSIONS

US Volume Measure	Metric Equivalent
⅛ teaspoon	0.5 milliliter
¼ teaspoon	1 milliliter
½ teaspoon	2 milliliters
1 teaspoon	5 milliliters
½ tablespoon	7 milliliters
1 tablespoon (3 teaspoons)	15 milliliters
2 tablespoons (1 fluid ounce)	30 milliliters
¼ cup (4 tablespoons)	60 milliliters
1/3 cup	90 milliliters
½ cup (4 fluid ounces)	125 milliliters
2/3 cup	160 milliliters
¾ cup (6 fluid ounces)	180 milliliters
1 cup (16 tablespoons)	250 milliliters
1 pint (2 cups)	500 milliliters
1 quart (4 cups)	1 liter (about)

WEIGHT CONVERSIONS

US Weight Measure	Metric Equivalent
½ ounce	15 grams
1 ounce	30 grams
2 ounces	60 grams
3 ounces	85 grams
¼ pound (4 ounces)	115 grams
½ pound (8 ounces)	225 grams
¾ pound (12 ounces)	340 grams
1 pound (16 ounces)	454 grams

OVEN TEMPERATURE CONVERSIONS

Degrees Fahrenheit	Degrees Celsius
200 degrees F	95 degrees C
250 degrees F	120 degrees C
275 degrees F	135 degrees C
300 degrees F	150 degrees C
325 degrees F	160 degrees C
350 degrees F	180 degrees C
375 degrees F	190 degrees C
400 degrees F	205 degrees C
425 degrees F	220 degrees C
450 degrees F	230 degrees C

BAKING PAN SIZES

American	Metric
8 x 1½ inch round baking pan	20 x 4 cm cake tin
9 x 1½ inch round baking pan	23 x 3.5 cm cake tin
11 x 7 x 1½ inch baking pan	28 x 18 x 4 cm baking tin
13 x 9 x 2 inch baking pan	30 x 20 x 5 cm baking tin
2 quart rectangular baking dish	30 x 20 x 3 cm baking tin
15 x 10 x 2 inch baking pan	30 x 25 x 2 cm baking tin (Swiss roll tin)
9 inch pie plate	22 x 4 or 23 x 4 cm pie plate
7 or 8 inch springform pan	18 or 20 cm springform or loose bottom cake tin
9 x 5 x 3 inch loaf pan	23 x 13 x 7 cm or 2 lb narrow loaf or pate tin
1½ quart casserole	1.5 liter casserole
2 quart casserole	2 liter casserole

INDEX